Drop Servicing

Building a Successful Drop Servicing Business

(All Inclusive Guide to Starting Your Drop Servicing Business and Creating Your Drop Servicing Website)

Erik Walker

Published By **Andrew Zen**

Erik Walker

Drop Servicing: Building a Successful Drop Servicing Business (All Inclusive Guide to Starting Your Drop Servicing Business and Creating Your Drop Servicing Website)

ISBN   978-1-998769-96-4

Legal & Disclaimer

The information contained in this ebook is not designed to replace or take the place of any form of medicine or professional medical advice. The information in this ebook has been provided for educational & entertainment purposes only.

The information contained in this book has been compiled from sources deemed reliable, and it is accurate to the best of the Author's knowledge; however, the Author cannot guarantee its accuracy and validity and cannot be held liable for any errors or omissions. Changes are periodically made to this book. You must consult your doctor or get professional medical advice before using any of the suggested remedies, techniques, or information in this book.

Upon using the information contained in this book, you agree to hold harmless the Author from and against any damages, costs, and expenses, including any legal fees potentially resulting from the application of any of the information provided by this guide. This disclaimer applies to any damages or injury caused by the use and application, whether directly or indirectly, of any advice or information presented, whether for breach of contract, tort, negligence, personal injury, criminal intent, or under any other cause of action.

You agree to accept all risks of using the information presented inside this book. You need to consult a professional medical practitioner in order to ensure you are both able and healthy enough to participate in this program.

Table Of Contents

Chapter 1: Drop Servicing

What is drop servicing?

To begin, I'd want to factor out that it's most possibly that you belong to considered one of two schooling. The first employer is constructed from individuals who are familiar with drop transport, at the equal time as the second organization is crafted from folks which might be clueless in this vicinity. If you are the numerous initial set of parents which is probably acquainted with drop delivery, then this need to be fairly sincere with the intention to do for the motive that the operational version is essentially the same. Even if you are peculiar with the concept of drop transport, the economic business agency model in the back of drop servicing ought want to be honest to understand. So, allow's begin through discussing the approach of drop servicing, we should? In its maximum fundamental shape, drop servicing may be described as a type of commercial enterprise organization version wherein the owner markets a business enterprise however pays every different party to offer it as an alternative. To pass a chunk similarly, you promote a service to your internet site;

however, you purchase the identical company from a person else who is selling it at a decrease price, and also you pocket the distinction among the price you charged for the issuer and the charge you paid for it. Service arbitrage is every other term that can be used to refer to drop servicing. You virtually carry in sales with the useful useful resource of performing as a pass-among in a corporation transaction that consists of the provision of services. You flow searching for services on freelancing internet net websites, wherein you can pay for them on call for, and then you definately absolutely promote the ones same offerings to potential corporations or customers that require the provider for 3 to five times the quantity that you pay the freelancer.

When you are making a sale, you visit the on-call for internet internet web page and look for a freelancer to rent so that they'll do the undertaking to your behalf.

Explain the distinction among drop servicing and drop shipping, further to the shared skills a number of the .

Drop transport and drop servicing are basically one-of-a-type names for the same organization exercising. Let's start with how the 2 are similar.

1.   In both state of affairs, you play the location of a middleman, selling a services or products that each other organization or individual is chargeable for providing. Imagine which you are a sales agent for someone or a organisation and that during alternate for locating clients for them, you get to function a markup to the rate and make a tidy earnings.

2.   You may additionally set up a worthwhile enterprise with little preliminary investment in case you want to interact in drop transport or drop servicing. You will need a completely little amount of cash whilst you don't forget that you may now not be required to make huge investments in any actual items or offerings, machinery, or other big investments.

three.   You may additionally additionally pick out out subjects up as you flow alongside. It isn't tough in any respect to get your drop shipping or drop servicing hold up and running, and as each day passes, you can make little changes depending at the information this is available to enhance your internet internet site and growth your earnings.

four.   Both drop servicing and drop delivery are low-threat business employer mind that you can check out. Because it calls for a touch time and financial dedication to carry out, the potential for loss on this company is pretty low.

5.   It is easy to comply the products and services your corporation gives to satisfy the requirements of growing marketplace tendencies and character clients. It isn't always tough to introduce new objects or services whilst the marketplace desires them for the reason that there may be no need to maintain any inventory and there may be no want to make massive fees in advance than doing so.

The following are the number one distinctions among drop servicing and drop delivery:

1.   The sale of offerings falls below the magnificence of drop servicing, even as the sale of bodily devices falls under drop shipping.

2.   Because the actual gadgets are sent right now to the purchaser thru the wholesaler or save from whom it changed into sold, you, as the vendor, do not have any contact with them at a few level within the drop shipping process. However, to workout drop servicing, you are required to gather the completed object or provider from the independent contractor and then supply it in your customer.

The blessings of drop servicing over drop delivery

Since we've got spent some of time discussing the parallels and versions among drop shipping and drop servicing, we want to speak about why drop servicing is advanced to drop transport. Permit me to demonstrate the belief of drop shipping and drop company via utilising the purple ocean and blue ocean framework, that is validated below in Figure 2.

Consider this: during the last numerous years, drop shipping has been extra well-known, and there may be now hundreds of companies that provide this company. Would you as a substitute compete to be the amazing drop shipper, or may additionally want to you as an alternative release a corporation using the identical industrial company version, but in a market that is as an opportunity new and has now not but been clearly exploited?

The second benefit of drop servicing is that it lets in you to boom a recognized carrier organization, and if you have a massive workload, you could even recruit freelancers on retainer or as whole-time employees of your business organization. This permits you to take advantage of the 0.33 benefit of drop servicing: Establishing your credibility as a dependable issuer of those services in your clients on this way will assist you domesticate prolonged-time period and fruitful agency connections.

The closing gain that drops servicing has over drop shipping is that it has far better margins than drop shipping does. If you have were given were given ever finished any business business enterprise research, you apprehend that earnings margins are the maximum crucial element of a corporation. The quantity of labor crucial is regularly the equal irrespective of whether or not or no longer you try and earn $1,000 by using the usage of using promoting a hundred goods which is probably every well surely really worth $10 item or via promoting one item that is well worth $1,000. Therefore, the maximum essential element is to optimize your earnings thru choosing the course of movement that consequences within the first-class feasible boom in margins of profits. When you do drop servicing, you often have more margins, and in case you've constructed up your employer and have a large extensive type of clients under your belt, you can even price higher charges while you don't forget that you may begin to restriction yourself to customers who have a better common price.

The benefits and drawbacks of drop servicing

Let's take a look at some of the benefits so that it will gift themselves to you when you release your very private drop servicing company.

Low startup fee

There isn't any want to make any sort of investment in your skillset to release a profitable drop-servicing corporation. You only need a crucial records of the carrier that you are imparting to reap fulfillment in this task. You furthermore may not want to make any vital investments in items or tool of any type, that could be a massive plus. Your most effective preliminary costs might be for the website that you create (which need definitely be a single net page if it absolutely is all you need) and the advertising which you do inside the first levels of your business enterprise.

Higher rate in line with sale

This is definitely one of the many blessings of the use of drop servicing. Because you're providing offerings, the charge regular with item will frequently be extra than it might be for matters which is probably normally used. The common rate for a service bouquet, relying on the cause marketplace, might in all likelihood variety anywhere from $ninety nine to $249. Because of this, a unmarried sale could probable deliver in a excellent earnings for you, but, the right quantity is predicated upon at the rate of the freelancer. In this bankruptcy there has been an mistakes; the stated supply couldn't be located. - There changed right into a hassle locating the reference supply. In this a part of the assessment, we appearance greater cautiously at the earnings and loss equation for drop servicing.

Recurring profits

When you operate drop servicing, it's miles noticeably easy to make certain which you have recurrent coins. When it involves the bulk of services, the clients need to preserve setting orders as a way to maintain their agency afloat. Consider the possibility of providing offerings such as layout for social media or content material fabric advertising offerings. The substantial majority of your customers will likely positioned you on a month-to-month retainer to maintain presenting those offerings to them.

Little abilties required

You simplest need to have a important expertise of the services which you are providing to get commenced out on the facet of your drop servicing corporation. You do now not need to realize how the carrier itself is completed; however, you do want to recognize what options are available to you and what form of the prevailing fee is for those options. The most beneficial problem of this is that you could look at it at the assignment. One distinct way to test it's miles which you have the choice of hiring a digital assistant who is informed in this location to address this for you if you do no longer sense comfortable discussing the technical additives of your corporation collectively along with your customers.

No transport or logistics danger

You won't must fear approximately the costs of transport or some other logistical headaches if you take gain of drop servicing. Because you are presenting a service, it's miles viable to offer them to clients over the internet, and there can be no want to address any physical devices. All that is required of you is data of the manner to manipulate the wonderful of the hobby that is delivered to you via your freelancer.

You may be incorrect if you idea that I may additionally want to actually highlight the powerful elements of drop servicing once I spoke to you approximately it. I am going to be very honest with you and let you realize that drop servicing isn't exactly a stroll in the park. The following are some of the drawbacks associated with drop servicing. However, in a few unspecified time within the future of this e-book, we are able to deal with each of those drawbacks as barriers for your business enterprise and make certain that you can meet your intention of incomes $1,000 to your first month as an entrepreneur within the drop carrier corporation.

1. Freelancer workload varies

When you have interaction in drop servicing, you'll be handling freelancers who aren't devoted to you and who can also moreover, as a end stop end result, have converting workloads, which may moreover reason the very last touch of your challenge to be behind schedule. You can also want to function a buffer timing to the transport timetable of the freelancer to reduce the possibility of this chance occurring.

2. Dealing with purchaser pleasure

When it involves dropping servicing, the delight of the clients is the single most essential trouble you could need to interest on. Because you probable do no longer want your client to be conscious which you are contracting out the assignment, this will be a tough state of affairs to navigate. Because of this, you have to handiest artwork with reliable freelancers who've excessive critiques.

In Chapter three.1, "Picking the Right Freelancer," we undergo in-intensity the way to locate and recruit the most certified freelancer, similarly to the way to make certain that they produce remarkable art work and stick with the remaining dates they've set.

For whom should drop carrier be most handy?

You are an brilliant candidate for drop servicing if you have as a minimum or 3 of the subsequent:

-       You do now not own any skills that is probably modified right into a worthwhile commercial enterprise or corporation.

-       Have talents that you can sell, but in place of doing the actual procedure your self, you choose to lease freelancers to do it for you so you can glide up the value chain.

-       Get comfortable with the concept of selling or advertising services which can be provided thru one of a kind humans.

-       very own awesome capabilities in customer support or challenge manipulate, and as a end quit result, can manage the outstanding of the offerings furnished by way of the use of approach of different oldsters.

- You need to make some money however you do not need to install as hundreds effort as it would take to perform the project.

- You need to carry out a provider-primarily based absolutely employer at the aspect or as a part of your entire-time assignment, but you do now not have a number of time or cash to spend money on getting it up and on foot.

- When beginning in the employer for the primary time, drop servicing is an great choice because it calls for little preliminary investment and, in most instances, most effective a touch quantity of a while.

After figuring out which you are as much as the challenge of being an expert drop servicing agent, permit's pass immediately to the following step of dissecting the economic company version and going via its many components.

The value chain for drop carrier provisioning

You are in all likelihood asking why it's so essential to have a awesome expertise of the fee chain of the drop-servicing agency. To positioned it each different manner, in case you characteristic a business corporation, the higher up the price chain you're, the loads lots much less probably it's miles that you'll be replaced through the use of every other employee. Because of this, it's far important to be able to be aware of your role inside the rate chain so you may match within the direction of carrying out the very best feasible tier interior it and therefore becoming your self more essential in your clients. To start our examination of the fee chain, allow us to don't forget a hooked up organisation which incorporates an straight forward internet keep (very much like a drop shipper). The devices are frequently offered via the store via a wholesaler, who acquired them from the producer in the first vicinity. The manufacturer furthermore makes use of raw substances derived from a number of specific property within the production of the object that it sells (see determine 3 that illustrates this). As you could see from the above instance, it can be as an alternative tough for a issuer company to preserve the complete cost chain of the goods. It isn't always hard the least bit for the purchaser to speak right away with the wholesaler in the event that they so want. The patron could possibly doubtlessly look for a top notch store that sells the identical product and method that save with a request for a discount or a few exclusive kind of fee addition that the store might be geared up to offer.

On the other hand, in case you act as a drop servicing agent, you are liable for the complete of the fee chain this is worried within the shipping of the carrier. This is because of the reality you control the connection that you have with the customer at once and the reality that you are the simplest character who is privy to the freelancer who performs the services that you supply your consumer. Because there is a ability for an impact at the output terrific, no purchaser ought to ever have the audacity to try to hire a freelancer on their non-public. Because it takes a freelancer a huge quantity of time to come back again to understand a customer's necessities, it's miles now not likely that a patron could be prepared to start instructing a current man or woman in the way wherein they may want their mission to be finished. As a give up end result, so long as you keep a immoderate diploma of first-rate inside the output of your output and produce on time, you'll be notable that you may have your customer for a huge amount of time.

Online advertising is the Way to move

In 2022, the best flow into you could make to your enterprise enterprise enterprise is to take it online. Because internet shopping is so on hand, brick-and-mortar stores are failing at an alarming charge. In 2020, I started out strolling within the place of virtual advertising and advertising. Inside simply five months, I had burned up most of my savings on advertising and the diverse quantities of software program utility I might want to launch a web organization. There grow to be not enough profits to maintain the employer going. After nearly emptying my bank account, I found about systeme.lo. Now that I've started out out my loose trial, I without a doubt have extra than sufficient bandwidth to renew working my net maintain. I'd learnt from my beyond mistake, and now I'm capable of generate earnings with little funding in infrastructure and oversight. Then I upgraded to the pinnacle magnificence model, and topics simply took off for my agency.

About Systeme.lo

In my opinion, systeme.Io is the best platform in which all the system vital to manipulate a flourishing internet agency may be determined in an one place. Before systeme.Io, it have become a huge trouble to installation a web employer due to the numerous services desired and the want to maintain track of several payments. Systeme.Io is an all-in-one answer for beginning, growing, and automating your net-based totally really enterprise. I'd want to specific my gratitude to Aurelian Amacker, the character in the back of this extraordinary internet site, for imparting content cloth cloth manufacturers, SMEs, and start-usalike ours with get admission to to great property without breaking the financial group. Because of its large series of pre-built additives, which includes launch templates, device, and automation, Systeme.Io streamlines the entire start-up procedure. Systeme.Io's pinnacle six skills are:

- Constructing a Sales Funnel

- Tools for electronic mail marketing and advertising

- Authoring Environment

- Creator of Websites

- Affiliate application manage

- Marketing automations

Having a sturdy net presence is feasible with most effective those gadget.

Reviewing Systeme.Io's Pros and Cons

No, I do no longer need you to agree with that the software is right. In my opinion, there are a few drawbacks to it as well.

Benefits

- An all-inclusive advertising and advertising device to which you could subscribe for a piece fee.

- It's a excellent way for green human beings to the world of net enterprise to get their feet wet for free of charge.

- A amazing get entry to element for logo spanking new companies into the digital market.

- The software program utility may be utilized by truely all of us with out a prior enjoy.

- The platform's pre-constructed templates may also moreover streamline your strategies notably.

- Inside the device, you could find out comprehensive courses approximately the use of it effectively and effectively.

- There is entire compatibility among all to be had equipment inside the gadget.

- The high-quality advantage is having everything you need to launch your net enterprise available from a unmarried hub.

- Thanks to automation software program program utility, your enterprise can feature even on the equal time as you're not there. The destiny chapters will bypass into further detail in this subject rely.

- Without the need to apprehend the manner to code, you may create your very own membership website on-line and on-line courses.

Drawbacks

- Without the use of Zapier, it isn't always feasible to attach any external app to the platform.

-       Advanced marketers can also war due to a lack of layout capabilities.

-       Because of its severa configuration picks, new customers can also need a while to come to be used to the platform.

-       The systeme.lo emblem may be protected within the footer of all emails and funnels despatched the usage of the unfastened version.

How To Use Systeme.lo?

Since you're definitely getting commenced out with systeme.lo, my aim in providing this documentation is to help you discover how the entirety works. Pay close to attention, thank you!

Sales Funnel Builder

Using the "create step" desire under the income funnel builder, you could acquire an Opt-in internet page, sales page, order shape, upsell internet net page, down promote web page, webinar web page, and exceptional pages to your advertising funnel. You may begin with a smooth slate or pick out out from some of examined, pre-designed templates for the shape of pages you need to create, making the profits funnel-building machine brief, easy, and simple.

When a touchdown net page template is chosen, the editor turns into a drag-and-drop interface. You also can customize a premade income funnel template or start from scratch with all of the device furnished. Your e-mail listing, rate processor, and membership net internet site also can all be related on your funnel for delivered performance.

Email Marketing Software

Two of the most not unusual abilties of email advertising and marketing software program software utility are the ability to format newsletters and electronic mail campaigns. Email layout may be completed the usage of either the visual or manual editor.

The time period "publication" refers to a unmarried e-mail that may be manually introduced in your e mail listing at a predetermined time.

The time period "marketing campaign" refers to a sequence of emails that you may create, time table, and supply on your touch listing.

The c language amongst e-mails might be spaced out to be minutes, hours, or maybe days. Clicking the "After" desire lets in you to choose an gift e-mail to supply the modern one after.

Course Creation Software

If you need to make guides the use of systeme.Io, you do no longer want to understand lots about era. Make a timetable to your direction and set up its modules. Create and amend lectures from interior your module. Course access have to be granted high-quality after receiving price via the platform's incorporated earnings channels and internet sites. All of your direction-related desires—development, merchandising, and earnings—can be met by means of way of manner of the usage of a single company.

The "Add scholar" preference allows you to deliver an electronic mail invitation to a selected man or woman. Give customers time to digest new fabric in advance than granting them get right of entry to to new modules with the Drip function.

Website Builder

Use a drag-and-drop internet site builder to create your ideal net website online as results as you'll a earnings funnel. Create a dependable weblog and publish frequently to keep readers interested.

Affiliate Management System

With the assist of an associate manipulate machine, you could recruit a legion of online promoters that will help you peddle your virtual wares to worried clients. Use the companion tracking software program to keep tabs on how a whole lot cash you're making out of your friends. Get your wares to be had on the systeme.Io market. Under the "partner software software settings" web page, you could regulate the affiliate fee %, Payment postpone, and payout threshold.

Marketing Automation Software

Rules and Workflows are the 2 number one sorts of advertising and marketing automation.

Certain responsibilities in a earnings funnel can be automatic with using automation pointers. It is possible to do that in a funnel. When a purchaser does a positive movement, like subscribing to a shape or seeing a particular web page, automation policies are brought on.

The favored motion to be fascinated about the useful resource of the person is listed after the reason. The image above depicts all of the capabilities that may be made available to clients. By doing so, you can programme your income funnel to run routinely.

To expand a very automated device, some of automation pointers (workflows) should be blanketed. Workflows include three awesome degrees. They are Action, Delays and Decision.

Action: When a customer plays an motion internal your funnel, you circulate them to the following available diploma on your technique.

Delays: It's feasible to assign a dispose of in time among two occasions.

As an instance, say you want a one-day pause amongst emails.

Decisions: Decisions are the numerous responses to clients' "Yes" or "no" votes.

Customers may be added to or eliminated from a marketing campaign based mostly on their moves, which includes clicking a hyperlink in an e-mail or now not.

The above technique diagram suggests how on this example, the customer fills out the subscription shape on "Home net net page 1," which then reasons the motion that sends the E-mail "Email 1" to the customer 30 days later. Clients are labeled as EN-Leads or no longer based totally on whether or no longer they do the motion of "Clicking the hyperlink" or not. This lets in you to time table matters to run mechanically, even while you are no longer round.

Chapter 2: Finding The Best

Independent Contractor

Identifying a Dependable Freelancer

As the gig economic gadget grows, freelancers play an increasingly large feature in workplaces in some unspecified time in the future of the globe. Thanks to Kolabtree, you can now hire a researcher or scientist for quick-time period or one-off assignments in addition to a agreement dressmaker or developer. It might be difficult to find and hire the appropriate freelancer on your art work. However, this isn't important. To assist you locate the correct candidate in your mission posting on Kolabtree, we've compiled this reachable advice.

Write a superb manner put up

Writing a concise pastime advert is the only approach to recruiting incredible and suitable applicants to your venture. To will let you find the most qualified freelancer, Kolabtree makes it short and easy to position up a technique and offer all applicable statistics. Pay close to attention to the following:

-        Project identify: The call of your undertaking need to include a succinct description of what you want. This will make it lots less complicated for freelancers to decide whether or not or now not or not they've the important skills to paintings for your project. Here's an excellent title for a venture: I want the services of a pharmacist who can create a cruelty-loose beauty product.

-        Project description: Be as unique as feasible even as describing your undertaking, and make sure to recognition on any understanding or enjoy the freelancer ought to own to do the work. Set down your venture's prevent motive and any planned outputs in element.

-        Duration: Define the expected length of the assignment and the reduce-off date for hiring simply so unbiased contractors might also additionally determine whether or no longer or no longer or now not they've got the time and belongings to take on the venture.

-        Budget: Specify how plenty coins you count on to need to finish the job. If you are not wonderful how a lot coins you will need, you could set a placeholder finances and negotiate a totally last price with impartial contractors. Add a be aware in your undertaking description in case you're inclined to barter. Both an hourly fee and a flat rate are available.

Shortlist freelancers

After amassing bids and recommendations, it might be difficult to select a unmarried organization in your mission. To find out the first rate freelancers with the right set of abilties to your challenge, it's far beneficial to create a shortlist. I'll inform you what you want to recognition on:

Proposal: Pay near interest to the freelancer's concept, in which they ought to element the task's predicted deliverables and deliver an purpose for why they need to be hired. Find out whether or not they have got revel in with jobs like yours and within the event that they have got the credentials you want for the position.

Profile: Check over the freelancer's Kolabtree profile and observe their preceding artwork and abilties. Look for publications that feature the expert as a frontrunner within the project even as the use of a researcher or scientist with a doctorate. Many of our independent contractors have advanced degrees of their fields of statistics; consequently, it's far crucial that you very well look at their resumes and areas of expertise.

Availability: Verify that the freelancer is to be had and has furnished a clean begin date for the project.

Interview shortlisted freelancers

• After narrowing down your preference of freelancers, you can have in-intensity conversations with them approximately your undertaking and pick the pleasant one. The software program itself allows for the scheduling of audio and video conferences. How to Have a Successful Interview

• Pick a on hand time: Since you can desire to paintings with a freelancer in a one-of-a-type time zone, it's far crucial to time desk conferences at a time this is handy for each of you.

• Prepare nicely: Ensure that you have examine the freelancer's idea thoroughly and characteristic a list of questions equipped to invite. Pose any questions you've got were given got, no longer only about the freelancer's experience and qualifications but also about the advised rate, to them.

•   Discuss the time table: Investigate how lengthy it might take to complete the mission's diverse deliverables and milestones. This is essential in keeping off frustrations and misunderstandings. If you are paying the freelancer hourly, you can ask that they preserve a timesheet for you. Make sure the freelancer is familiar with some time constraints.

Should I Just Go with the Lowest Bidder on a Freelancer Service?

How Much to Charge for Your Services as a Freelance Programmer, and Why You Should Not Offer the Lowest Rates?

This is why it's far tempting to undervalue your services as a freelancer.

Especially as a newbie to a community like Fiverr, it might be tempting to try to undercut the opposite developers via giving a absolutely cheap price in your services.

It's the first-class manner to win over a customer, proper?

For what it is well really worth, if you've arrived at this end, recognize that you're in right business enterprise: lots upon plenty of other builders have arrived on the same end.

The unpleasant impact is a state of affairs that exists these days on the various most distinguished freelancing net web sites: a charge struggle.

There's no point in you, the freelancer, gambling this pastime.

Whenever you're running for pennies on the greenback, you are in a hurry to get as a brilliant deal done as feasible in as little time as feasible (you do must feed your family, right?). As a effect, the very last product can be of decrease first-class.

Potentially unfavourable in your expert reputation, which might also purpose the shortage of destiny artwork or, not plenty much less than, the lack of potential to price more in your subsequent interest.

This is a excessive aspect in why we are not the lowest-priced developer to be had. There are, but, some greater that we are going to have a have a examine in detail beneath.

In cease of this, I want you to agree with me that a "Race to the Bottom" is a lousy concept. Instead, I need to depart you encouraged and armed with the assets to interrupt out or keep away from adopting a "permit me actually be the cheapest" mentality.

When jogging as a freelancer, it's miles not an great concept to compete on price.

Cease the Destruction of Values and Standards

What we call a "Race to the Bottom" takes place whilst many independent contractors bid at the identical mission. In evaluation to standard bidding, freelancers frequently outbid one greater by using manner of presenting ever-lower fees till a hard and fast floor is finished.

This method that a patron can also moreover exceptional pay you a couple of bucks for a device that takes you masses hours to perform.

Many on-line freelancing web sites are worldwide; for this reason, the rate of a dollar varies significantly depending on in that you stay.

Depending on in which you pass, one dollar may additionally moreover or won't buy you a superb meal.

Freelancers honestly beginning in areas with excessive living prices, alongside facet the European Union (EU), the usa (US), and similar regions regularly forget about this. People the usage of a freelancing net website online can also mistakenly be given as true with they want to provide certainly the lowest rate possible. They endure in mind this to be their great alternative for purchasing their first venture belief permitted.

In regions similar to the European Union, wherein the dollar travels substantially farther than in the United States, a freelancer may also discover herself going for walks at a loss on each project they take shipping of.

This is an hassle.

Customers Consider Your Services a Generic Good

A freelancer will generally provide an hourly price whilst imparting their offerings to a customer. If you're taking this tack, your customer also can decide to pick out a wonderful freelancer who gives their services at a lesser rate.

Because of this, charging through the usage of the hour is bigoted to each you and your purchaser.

If you are a freelancer seeking out more paintings, you'll be tempted to offer lower hourly expenses. This may encourage brilliant freelancers to do the identical.

Customers seeking out a freelancer will do exactly that: search around.

One of the problems with charging with the aid of the hour is that it maintains you in a pricing battle with competitors, however any other is that it prevents you from displaying a capacity consumer the real price you could offer to their enterprise.

You need to rethink your pricing method altogether if you do not need your clients to deal with your knowledge like a few other provider they may get for the cheapest viable rate according to hour.

Advice on a way to avoid making a horrible freelancer rent

Freelancers are regularly inexperienced and price range nice. They show there, do what has to be completed, and then pass. There's an excessive amount of paperwork and obligation involved with hiring a whole-time worker, and you do no longer have the time to cope with it anyways.

However, irrespective of the reality that this may sound like a business proprietor's dream come genuine, there can be one large hassle to be had: fantastic. Sadly, many freelancers, even those with a extremely good tune file of getting jobs and great scores, emerge as delivering subpar artwork when they get their palms for your cash.

Here are 5 precautions you need to take to choose out a freelancer at the manner to deliver as promised and keep away from this nightmarish scenario:

1.   Use many excellent structures.

The number one purpose of your pastime posting must be to attract as many unbiased contractors as feasible.

Even despite the fact that there are tens of tens of millions of freelancers available, you can't get as many responses on your task posting as you'll count on. This is mainly the case at the identical time as belongings are restricted or whilst unusual records is needed.

You may additionally find freelancers on severa web sites committed to that reason. You'll have get proper of entry to to a broader pool of capability applicants from which to pick the great one.

2.   please maintain off on making that hiring for some days.

You should not rush into hiring the number one to be had freelancer who meets your desires. Somebody else, without a doubt as in a feature however extra low price, can also come alongside in a few days and make you an offer.

There are times on the same time as you in fact want to get some issue accomplished by way of way of using a selected time. If it definitely is the case, you can ought to settle with a much less-than-ideal candidate.

You may additionally moreover moreover keep away from this catch 22 situation by using way of marketing a system starting earlier than you are confident you could have a gap. I would no longer do it very regularly for the cause that it's far cheating, but the solution is sure. However, there may be no penalty for a one-time use of this approach if it consequences to your not using a person to do the paintings.

three.   Find out their enjoy in comparable roles via using task interviews with the top opportunities.

There is a good judgment at the back of why most agencies simplest interview candidates for complete-time positions in character. Most independent contractors will not be open to assembly with you in man or woman, however a brief phone chat or Skype session must suffice.

Candidates' information of the placement's requirements can be gauged through talk. Demand samples in their previous art work and provide them with times of the necessities you have got got for a employed hand.

Don't differentiate them from whole-time candidates.

four. Make your prospects comply with a few easy commands as a take a look at.

As a community, we despise direct mail emails, and freelancing systems are notorious for his or her abundance. Freelancers every now and then comply with to many commercials with the same creation and cover letter. These unbiased contractors in all likelihood have now not given your hobby marketing the attention it merits and isn't an superb in form.

This devious method can be used to weed out ability spammers: Include a difficult and fast of commands inside the center of your article for you to permit you to tell whether or now not a candidate examine everything. To show that they have got examine the complete posting, you could consist of the road "I've really look at your positioned up" in your manner description.

Additionally, that is a tremendous technique for casting off applicants who can not or won't have a look at recommendations.

5. Divide the artwork into feasible quantities.

It remains viable to rent a person inept, even if you take every precaution indexed above.

Sadly, I actually have to tell you that that could be a common incidence. Where do you draw the road at the same time as this worst-case scenario happens?

To accomplish extra, divide large duties into potential chunks. It is not unusual workout to encompass a listing of relevant "milestones" in a hobby commercial enterprise.

Once your freelancer reaches a certain milestone, they may report lower lower back to you. You are free to right away terminate the settlement if you are sad with the effects.

It stays essential to compensate the freelancer for completed work, however the overall quantity owed may be far lower than it'd had been in any other case. What's extra, it'll provide you with greater time to select a freelancer who can supply amazing results.

Chapter 3: If I Desired To Begin A Corporation, What Offerings May Want To You Advise I Sell?

What makes selecting a specialization so essential to your fulfillment?

Now that you are organized to generate cash on-line together together with your drop servicing industrial company, step one is to select which services you need to provide to customers to maximise your profits. We advise which you make a decision the exceptional market niche to your organisation earlier than locating out which services you want to offer to capability customers. You can be asking your self why it is important to pick out out a specialization to your commercial employer rather than genuinely selling any offerings that might be supplied. You can also moreover earn a exceptional amount of cash doing this, but your earnings margins may no longer be as high as they'll be if you specialized in a unmarried area. This is the first reason why being a "jack of all crafts and draw near of none" isn't a great advertising strategy for you. Keep in thoughts that the profit margin is particularly critical in the company. To refresh your memory, we went over this case rely in phase 1.6, wherein we spoke about how one of the advantages of drop servicing is the prolonged profit margin which you may have because of using this method. Second, there may be awesome fee in being an professional in a sure subject. Permit me to offer an reason of using the example of a health practitioner. The commonplace profits of a famous practitioner in 2019 come to be a decent $237,000, that is a big upward push from the preceding diploma of $195,000 (a 21 percent increase). On the alternative hand, the commonplace earnings for professionals has been continuously more than that of primary care physicians, and it has extended from $284,000 in 2015 to $341,000 (an boom of 20 percent). This brings the total to $341,000. (Kane, et al., 2020). Please are seeking for recommendation from determine four for an instance.

You are probably asking what the pay of specialized physicians has to do with drop servicing. I can see why that might be the case. The idea that a specialized medical doctor ought to make an profits this is forty three percent greater than that of a fashionable physician is what I am looking for to get throughout to you. In a comparable vein, as a drop servicing agent, your income is probably confined if you are a jack of all crafts. On the alternative hand, if you give attention to a high-quality location, you will be able to fee better charges, so you can notably enhance your margins.

You can be capable of have an area of information wherein you may end up a professional after you have got were given picked your area of expertise; this will will allow you to become an expert in that area. Choosing a gap will let you make alternatives at the form of services and products you'll provide, the varieties of clients you can pursue and try to win over, and the independent contractors you may hire.

When you select out an opening, it does not continuously endorse that you need to consciousness on a pretty specific subcategory or subject of understanding. The majority of internet companies, in my revel in, pick out out a massive vicinity of information, then 0 in on a specific aspect of this capability place to pay interest their efforts on and emerge as an expert. Permit me to complicated in this factor with an example. The following desk presents some instances of diverse kinds of location of interest specializations which is probably to be had.

At the very top, we provide 4 (4) one-of-a-kind opportunities for niches, and under each opportunity, we include some instances of specializations that fall inner that precise niche. Consequently, the technique which you want to do is to pick a specialty inner an opening after which offer offerings that are centered on the chosen information.

The exceptional detail is that there are heaps upon masses of niches available, and you can need to pick out a powerful vicinity of interest which you are comfortable jogging internal. The single most substantial trouble that we educate on this eBook is that as opposed to searching for to function in numerous niches proper away, you need to pick out one location of interest and offer specialized services inner that location of hobby instead of spreading yourself too skinny through seeking to function in multiple niches right now.

The following are some of the benefits that consist of identifying to create a specialised organisation in choice to a favored one.

1.   It lets in you to consciousness your efforts on a specific area of expertise, this is beneficial.

2.   Customers like dealing with specialists due to the fact they are certain they can depend upon the art work this is produced through the ones experts.

three.   You can be able to offer your organization with a clean path for setting up your advertising and advertising and marketing plan to collect immoderate-paying clients thanks to this possibility.

4.   Your advertising message can be simplified, and you'll be able to take gain of economies of scale thinking about you may now not be required to sell each company separately.

five.   Allows you to shorten the time it takes to get your first purchaser as it simplifies the way via manner of manner of which ability clients also can understand your business employer as an skilled company and, as a stop end result, choose to turn out to be a paying customers. In the subsequent paragraph, we will talk in further detail the manner you want to pick out a profitable specialized market wherein to launch your commercial enterprise corporation.

Our Suggested Method for Choosing Specific Markets

Evaluate both your interests and your abilties.

This won't appear like loads, but believe me as quickly as I say that it has a sizeable effect. Do not choose a niche certainly due to the fact you are "kind of involved" in it; as an alternative, for it to be sustainable, it want to as a substitute be some component that you could picture yourself being captivated with for as a minimum 5 years.

Is this something which you like doing for your spare time or a few thing that you may preserve to do even when you have been not being paid for it?

This will be an extremely good desire for the market that you operate in.

Consider which fields you have were given specialized expertise or understanding in whilst you recall that this is some other crucial consideration to make. What are a number of the matters that awesome people frequently reward you on? Where did you get your education or schooling? What unique abilties or specialised know-how have you ever ever ever received because of your art work?

When searching out your niche, the sweet spot is even as you discover a scenario which you are informed approximately and which you even have a passion for. This emerge as some element that I did with my productiveness calendar, and I decided that it labored out incredibly nicely for me.

There are severa outstanding departures from this preferred norm. To offer you with an example, truly one of my earliest firms changed into promoting garage containers for Christmas trees. I wasn't exactly obsessed with the product, however I modified into obsessed with going for walks a a success enterprise corporation and assisting my goal marketplace in finding the right solution for his or her needs.

Determine whether or not or no longer or no longer there is a need for the goods or services that fits your area of interest.

Unfortunately, having a strong hobby in a fine project isn't always enough (how I need it have been!).

You want to moreover test to look whether or now not or now not there is a need for it; if there isn't, your hobby will live a hobby instead of growing right into a financially worthwhile corporation agency.

Simple studies on relevant key phrases is a top notch area to start at the same time as trying to understand the organization. For this motive, the Google Keyword Planner is a very beneficial device.

Put in a few key phrases which may be relevant on your specialised area, after which test the recommended phrases and terms.

Reduce the big sort of tips through taking into consideration the month-to-month are searching out extent, the quantity of opposition, and the proposed provide.

Regarding the amount of searches, keep to amongst 1,000 and 10,000 each month. If it's far some distance lower than this big variety, there normally isn't an lousy lot of a marketplace for it; if it's far considerably higher, it is able to be too tough to rank in Search.

When it involves competitiveness, low to medium is the way to move. Even on the identical time as this simplest gives records approximately how aggressive the time period or word is in AdWords and no longer herbal search; it is able to even though provide you with a vital indication of the tiers of natural opposition.

When it includes the proposed provide, bids which may be greater than the minimum amount regularly mirror a high degree of business purpose. Therefore, huge bids frequently imply that customers are willing to pay greater fees for the motive that they profit greater when they rank for such key phrases.

Narrow down your aim marketplace.

At this diploma, you may need to do not forget making your intention market even extra particular. For example, you can have determined that "freelance writing" is a famous region of hobby; despite the fact that, you will be inquisitive about identifying whether or not or not or now not or no longer you may find out a focus in your area of interest that is even extra unique.

Visiting applicable communicate forums, Facebook groups, and subreddits is one of the most effective strategies to perform this motive.

You might also moreover furthermore decide which subtopics or sub-niches you is probably interested in pursuing thru using a device like Redditlist. Simply input your number one key phrases into the hunt bar, after which browse the most famous subreddits to peer if any of them pique your hobby.

Explore this assignment in further depth by way of the use of going to those subreddits, at the aspect of various specialised businesses and forums, to discover which subject topics or questions are cited often. This might also moreover assist you higher define your niche (as an instance, "freelance era fiction authors"), and it can moreover assist you come up with unique sub-niches or mind for blog placed up topics for the future.

Examine the alternative contenders to be had in the marketplace for your self.

Researching key terms is important, however you want to additionally inspect the extent of competition for your unique region. This is a few factor you need to do for your personal.

Try entering a number of the terms you've got located into Google and seeing which web web sites display up at the number one web page of effects. You will encounter one of the following:

1.   There are already a incredible style of well-known web sites competing for the ones keywords in the are seeking for effects. This precise specialized market may be already quite competitive, wherein case you could try to find out one which isn't always almost as famous.

2.   There aren't any net web sites that rank for such key phrases at this time.

3.   Be careful on this regard; in spite of the fact that this could imply that there is lots of possibilities, it more likely method that others have already identified that this unique marketplace segment does now not exist.

4.   There are a few web sites that rank for sure key phrases; but, in famous, they're both very tiny or of terrible first-rate.

five. This is a usually high-quality indicator that this specialised marketplace need to be pursued. This specialized marketplace probable has some capability customers, and the level of competition won't be too severe.

Congratulations! You have now determined on a selected market phase and investigated the available options in that section. Now is the immediate to discover whether or not or not or now not this particular marketplace phase is without a doubt as profitable and famous as you had was hoping it'd be.

Test your vicinity of hobby

Even if the market research you've got previously completed is beneficial, not anything beats placing your services or products to the test within the real worldwide to appearance whether or now not you are heading in the first-rate path.

Creating a touchdown web page that advertises a loose information product this is linked to your region of hobby is one method you could use to check your subject matter earlier than you positioned up an entire net website online devoted to it. Using a platform together with Leadpages makes this technique quite simple.

Next, use AdWords to direct traffic to the touchdown web web page you have created. This will offer you the functionality to determine how a superb deal hobby there honestly is to your region of interest and/or product and could display you ways an lousy lot hobby there's in phrases of internet site traffic and downloads. Keep in mind that during case you are receiving a whole lot of web site traffic from AdWords however not many conversions, the problem is often with the material for your touchdown net web page in place of the vicinity of hobby itself.

Surveying your goal market is another method for validating your uniqueness. You want to promote it your survey anywhere which you have interaction collectively along side your aim marketplace, along with on your vacationer posts, in agencies regarding your sector, on social media, via Google surveys (you could pay Google to sell the ones for you), and so forth.

You want to now revel in confident (or no longer!) in building up your robust point internet site and social media money owed, given what you have got got determined through your PPC sorting out and surveys.

However, in case you do now not sense self perception, it's far k.

Conclusions and musings

Even whilst following this five-step technique may not make sure your success in your selected area, it must offer you with some idea and a strong basis upon which to bring together. In addition to this, it's going to assist in mitigating the risks related to launching a place of information internet internet web page, so saving you time, coins, and frustration.

How can I apprehend whether or not or no longer or not the market section I've chosen is profitable?

How to Determine whether or not Your Specialty Market is Going to Be Successful

Consider your specialization while launching an associate marketing enterprise. Your commercial enterprise's fulfillment will rely upon its specialization. A niche is a marketplace vicinity with unique services or gadgets to reply a specific need. Large niches may be divided into smaller sub-niches. Half of affiliate advertising and marketing and advertising and marketing web sites fail because of the fact they lack a region of statistics. Your commercial employer's specialization must be rewarding for long-term achievement.

How to determine an opening's profitability. You'll keep away from half the trouble other net web sites or companies face in advance than failing. Taking too prolonged to pick out a robust factor may be annoying. Paralysis via analysis may additionally take place.

Do ok have a look at to locate useful niches. You might also moreover be part of the market quicker and with extra impact. First topics first.

Identify Your Passion

First, find out a beneficial location of interest. Discover your interests and pastimes.

You've in reality taken into consideration this in case you're constructing a net web web page or internet business enterprise. If no longer, set up a listing of 10 property you are obsessed on and can convert right into a agency.

Running a agency is tough and turns into difficult. Only a actual interest for your artwork can get you via hard times. It's in particular real for first-time entrepreneurs.

Consider your interests and brilliant interests. Repeatedly performing a few element can also unconsciously assemble talent or information.

Passion obligations won't be beneficial, so make a list. Find a topic you could immerse your self in and monetize.

Ascertain Niche Market Value

After figuring out potential profitable niches, determine their market nicely well worth. You need to understand the location of interest's price before getting into it. The region of hobby's market worth will allow you to understand how an lousy lot you may make. If the marketplace charge is high, you could in all likelihood find out a place of hobby.

Online, there are various lists illustrating marketplace areas' in reality virtually well worth. They display the internet rate of various marketplace regions. If you cannot compute a niche's marketplace properly worth, it may be too tiny or there wasn't sufficient information. You must now not enter the region of hobby because you cannot expect its profitability.

Check Past and Current Patterns

Before leaping right right into a specialization, analyze all you can. Past and gift market styles can tell you lots about it. Checking specialised market traits has in no way been a whole lot less tough. Search Google Trends for your place.

Google lists all net niches. They provide loose, correct information.

You need a niche that has been and is strong. Seasonal niches are fads and not worthwhile. Check ten-yr traits and styles. If you can, go farther.

Identify Problems to Solve

To gain achievement, your place of interest need to offer a choice to a trouble faced by way of the use of the folks who will buy your service or product. To a outstanding volume, your business agency's achievement or failure will rely upon how nicely you address the desires of your motive marketplace phase. Considering your skills to deal with market troubles is essential. There is a call for for even the most outlandish thoughts.

Talking to participants of your target audience may additionally assist you discover ache elements. Create some studies questions on the way to show whether or not or now not this marketplace is virtually well worth pursuing. Also, take a look at out on line discussion forums to peer if there are commonplace problems that want fixing that you can help others with. You also can look at masses from humans's open debates about problems on internet web sites like Quora.

Searching Google's most famous terms is each specific method for locating issues that need solving. You may study plenty from the findings approximately what people are actively seeking out on-line and whether or not or no longer or now not it is probably rewarding to provide them with solutions.

If you could provide an authentic, floor-breaking way to an contemporary problem, you may determine to enter a crowded niche.

Find Products or Services to Sell

There is an trouble available, and in case you endure in thoughts you realise the way to restore it, there is a selected market in your services or products. The next step is to provide a method to the problem, which you can marketplace to clients. The first-class and most worthwhile markets are those who have a massive variety of every tangible and digital items. Even if there can be only a restrained market to your objects, you'll be able to make masses of cash.

Internet marketing is a excellent example of an opening marketplace as it functions a massive sort of agencies and probably lots of items. All you need is some form of evidence that a huge style of clients within the place of hobby make purchases.

Whether you want to apprehend if there are devices to sell in a fantastic area, you should have a take a look at companion advertising networks.

To studies what is doing properly in certain submarkets, you can peruse partner packages similar to the ones furnished with the useful resource of marketplaces like eBay, Amazon, and Click bank.

One specific splendid useful aid for learning about a product is a drop delivery net net website online.

In addition, many internet web sites might also have sub-niches internal your area of interest, further segmenting the marketplace. To offer one instance, the sports activities activities activities and fitness area of interest is in addition subdivided into sub-niches like walking, swimming, yoga, and others. In addition, they will price the pinnacle-promoting gadgets, so you can manual you to the topics in an effort to promote brilliant.

Check Reviews

Products on marketplaces like Amazon and eBay always have man or woman reviews from a big fashion of clients. They may be an important a part of gauging the potential fulfillment of your specialized concept. One trouble you can have regarding the vicinity of interest that evaluations may additionally furthermore assist you with is whether or now not or not or now not the target marketplace is ready to pay for the property you are presenting. You have to are searching for merchandise for which the response is strong.

Customers' propensity to spend cash is outstanding examined via manner of manner of objects that have acquired several favorable evaluations. The quantity of reviews subjects really as thousands due to the fact the exceptional of those critiques in phrases in their percent. Only an first-rate product can get hundreds of five-massive name ratings on internet web sites like Amazon and eBay.

How an entire lot are you capable of charge for this?

Pricing your services competitively to usher in clients and make a income.

J.D. Candidate Stephen Fishman's unique art work. Payment for the art work of an IC may also additionally take numerous office work, at the side of a flat rate for the whole project an hourly fee, or a percentage of profits. Whether you rate customers hourly, in step with deliverable, or for the whole challenge, you could need to determine your costs first. Knowing how many hours the undertaking will take and your preferred hourly salary can assist making a decision on a fair steady fee. If you have got got worked to your career for a while, you possibly have an super idea of what your costs should be. On the alternative hand, You may not apprehend what type of expenses to ask for whilst you're genuinely starting. If this is your cutting-edge-day scenario, then use those steps to get your hourly fee:

- Work out your price relying on your prices.

- Find out what the modern-day marketplace fee is and whether or no longer you need to alternate it.

Figure Out How Much You're Making Per Hour

There is a popular method for calculating an hourly profits this is taught in agency instructions: Calculate your hourly income by means of using multiplying your selected earnings through your average difficult work and overhead prices. This is the lowest possible charge while even though defensive all of your costs, which incorporates an less expensive earnings for your self. You can be capable of indict greater or an entire lot less on your offerings, relying on present day marketplace situations.

Find out how masses coins you may be making every 3 hundred and sixty five days. Decide on a every yr repayment to estimate the price of your services. You also can base this on what you made in a previous interest doing comparable artwork, what one-of-a-kind humans are presently making in comparable jobs, or what you observed you are sincerely really worth (as long as your aim is much less high priced).

Calculate the every yr overhearing.

The next step is to figure out your every year fees. All costs that aren't immediately associated with generating a product or providing a organization are considered overhead.

-    costs related to making phone calls

-    Equipment, furnishings, and utilities for the place of business things like stationery and administrative center materials

-    liberation charges

-        • clerical useful useful resource • industrial organization insurance • inside the context of agency, a meal, and some mild entertainment

-    spending money on a adventure

-        Membership in a Professional Organization

Advertising and marketing charges, together with the fee of a net internet site on-line exchange gambling playing cards, or leaflets and crook and accounting services.

•• Your profits taxes and self-employment taxes, further to the charge of your fringe advantages like scientific medical health insurance, incapacity coverage, and retirement blessings, also are taken into consideration overhead.

Starting, you may need to make informed guesses about those prices or studies what similar ICs to your vicinity spend in overhead in advance than making any financial picks.

Pick out a margin of earnings.

You need to moreover be capable of make coins after paying yourself and any critical overhead. To positioned it really, your earnings is a vital enterprise business enterprise cost that cannot be deducted from the bottom line. Earning a earnings is the payoff for going into organisation for your private. It offers you the capital you need to assemble and increase your employer. Profit is regularly stated as a percentage of charges. A earnings of 10% to twenty% is conventional, on the identical time as there may be no set benchmark.

Count up the hours to look how an lousy lot you may price.

The closing step is to calculate your annual profits based totally totally on the enormous type of hours you advise to paintings. For the sake of this computation, allow's assume you'll paintings 40 hours each week, no matter the fact that you can wind up putting in more. There is an annual cap of ,000 billable hours, which equates to a single - week tour. (50 weeks x forty hours). There may be much less time to be had for billing abilities in case you plan on taking an prolonged tour.

Of course, you'll spend somewhere among 25 and 35 percentage of it gradual on non-billable sports activities like accounting and billing, networking, and competencies improvement. If you continue to desire a - week excursion consistent with 12 months, this indicates you can in all likelihood satisfactory be capable of artwork 1,three hundred to at least one,500 hours for pay.

Example

Sam, a self-hired internet site style dressmaker, believes he's entitled to at the least the same annual sales as an IC as he had whilst he changed into an employee ($a hundred,000). He estimates that $20,000 in keeping with twelve months may be essential to assist his costs of living. He plans to paintings sort of 1,500 billable hours in step with yr and hopes to make a 10% profits. Sam involves a decision his hourly charge as follows:

-      He calculates his universal profits and charges as follows: $100,000 + $20,000 Equals $one hundred and twenty,000.

-      Then he is taking the sum and multiplies it by using the usage of his income margin of 10% in advance than which include in his pay and exclusive agency charges: When finished to $a hundred twenty,000, 10% is $12,000, consequently $100 and twenty,000 plus $12,000 is $132,000.

-      Finally, he calculates his hourly charge through the usage of dividing the every yr sum via way of his billable hours: $132,000 1,500 = $88.

Sam makes $90 an hour (rounded up). Sam may be capable of fee more, or he may additionally moreover must take delivery of a decrease charge, relying on the country of the marketplace.

Investigate the Marketplace

If you need to earn greater than just an hourly salary, you want to do extra than simply the mathematics. If you're considering this quantity, you want to additionally recollect whether or now not or now not it's far sensible. As a cease result, you want to research the going rate for your offerings and the prices charged with the aid of competing ICs. There is a plethora of sources to be had to help you accumulate this information.

You need to get in touch with a alternate agency or professional company on your area of information. It might be of provider in letting you apprehend what community ICs are charging.

- Find out the going fee from similar ICs. You can also additionally talk price problems with one in all a kind ICs on line.

- Visit trade events and corporate gatherings to network with searching for what you provide.

- Salary.Com, Glassdoor, and PayScale are just a few websites that could give you an concept of what different companies pay for similar paintings.

You might also moreover determine that your remarkable hourly charge is extra than the going charge for ICs on your place. Nonetheless, if you're certified and doing exquisite art work, you have to no longer be afraid to rate extra than splendid ICs. Customers is probably have become off thru excessively cheap costs. Many potential customers accept as true with that you get what you pay for, and are willing to spend greater for pinnacle-notch products or services.

One method is to start charging a fee that is at the low quit of the variety for ICs offering the equal or similar offerings, and then little by little growth it till rate resistance is encountered. With some trial and errors, you need to be able to choose a technique of fee and fee of compensation that brings in enough paintings and sufficiently rewards your efforts.

Make a Written Fee Agreement

After choosing pricing with a consumer, it's far crucial to have a written price settlement in region. (If you will instead have a hard and speedy rate for the whole interest, virtually multiply the kind of hours you estimate the paintings will take through your hourly price of preference.)

When selling my business business organisation, how masses need to I expect to pay for commercials?

Online advertising and advertising has made it less difficult than ever to extend your organisation's consumer base. However, there is lots to soak up, and for parents which is probably new to net marketing and advertising and marketing, it might be a bit overwhelming.

Ad layouts, marketing campaign kinds, and commonplace performance statistics may also additionally additionally range extensively throughout particular net advertising systems. But underlying the entirety is the perennial inquiry.

"What is the fee tag on this?"

We're going to transport deep into the advertising and marketing budgets of the three crucial on line advertising and marketing and advertising and marketing networks today: Google AdWords, Facebook Ads, and Instagram.

We'll test the professionals and cons of each online advertising and advertising platform, as well as the variations in advertising and marketing prices, amongst Google, Facebook, and Instagram. Finally, we are going to compare and evaluation the respective typical performance of each platform, drawing on large number one resources and empirical evidence.

On short summarise our manual to net advertising and advertising and marketing fees, we are able to say the following:

-     On commonplace, a click on-via from a are in search of for network ad on Google Ads (AdWords) may additionally need to set you lower lower back $2.32. On the Display Network, the regular CPC is a lot much less than $0.Fifty eight.

-         Google marketing are seeking for campaigns typically have a CPA of $59.18.

-     In every Google AdWords and Bing Ads, the very first-rate-call for are searching for terms also can command CPCs of $50 or extra.

- These are regularly extraordinarily competitive key terms in businesses which have big customer lifetime values, along with law and coverage.

- Small organizations that use Google AdWords commonly pay among $9,000 and $10,000 monthly on their advertising and marketing campaigns. That's a each 12 months earnings of $one hundred,000 to $a hundred and twenty,000.

- Typically, advertisers pay spherical $1.Seventy for every click on a Facebook advert. Ads on Facebook generally have a CPC of $18.Sixty eight.

- Ads on Facebook generally have a price consistent with thousand impressions (CPM) of spherical $10.

- While the not unusual price constant with thousand impressions (CPM) for an Instagram ad is now within the direction of $5, this range is predicted to rise because the net website keeps to benefit reputation.

How excessive is opposition in my precise location?

Wondering the manner to find out the maximum useful niches with little competition? Curious about techniques for identifying new topics and developing your partner sports? In this educational, we walk you through the exquisite strategies and procedures for identifying your next affiliate project.

Google Trends is a terrific device for discovering and investigating superb niches.

By reading Google Trends, you could discover untapped markets with little to no competition and excessive ability income. With issues for time, area, and language, it examines how often used Google are attempting to find terms are. Using this tool, you may see how certain are seeking for phrases and subjects have grown or declined in reputation over the years.

Using this approach, you could find out each perennially-thrilling and freshly-trending niches, further to gauge the capability of a extraordinary project to be used in destiny advertising campaigns. If you're looking for a low-competition location of interest, cross no further than our whole educational on the use of Google trends.

Find markets to take benefit of in a exceptional situation.

Finding low-competition, excessive-income niches can also be finished via specializing in sub-markets that lend themselves to masses of monetization techniques. This permits you beautify profitability and capability earnings.

Having plenty of methods to monetize your content material fabric now not best increases your sales capability however additionally reduces the possibility that your earnings may also dry up. In case one technique of getting cash from your content cloth stops operating, you have got every different prepared to go.

To make coins in a sturdy point, you want to consider the subsequent questions.

-        Exactly what are the maximum widespread techniques of being worthwhile on this particular difficulty?

-        How well does this method mesh collectively together with your marketing blueprint?

-     What shape of accomplice packages are there on your specific market?

Make a word of the numerous monetization techniques you could find out on fantastic web sites that appear to accumulate this region. Is there any proof of online show advertising on their website on line? Where would possibly the associate hyperlinks be? How do they make cash, precisely?

It's vital to hold an eye out for a good deal less apparent techniques of monetization, which consist of newsletters and gated material inside the people' segment. Sign up for them to try them out.

Collect records approximately all accomplice programs which can be relevant to that marketplace. Find out what forms of commissions are ordinary in that location. Do you receives a commission commissions frequently, or is this a one-time deal? Determine what your normal fee will be. When reading affiliate applications in a given field, it is probably beneficial to ask yourself the following questions:

-    Just what number of amazing associate applications are there to choose out out from?

-    How do their bills paintings exactly? Do you gets a commission often, or is it a one-time deal?

-     How excellent is the payoff, normally speakme? Work up a ballpark determine for the identical old rate percentage.

Analyzing the Competition in Terms of Search Volume and Difficulty

The approach of reading the opposition is vital even as searching out worthwhile niches with less competition. Conducting an in-depth evaluation of the opposition is critical for understanding the profitability of a market and your function internal it. Researching how prolonged it takes to rank for a positive area of interest or phrase with pretty some competition is vital to the fulfillment of your time-honored method.

To prevail, one must find out a market segment that isn't surely with out competition. Niches with pretty little opposition generally suggest a bad possibility for monetization and profitability.

Techniques for assessing slim markets with a hint rivalry

Several metrics may be used to gauge how tough it's miles to achieve achievement in a certain region. Using a software program software application like Semrush or Ahrefs is the extremely good desire. Look at the important component-word problem, charge regular with click on, and are trying to find volumes for the widest key phrases in a gap.

The issue of a term to rank for is represented by way of manner of severa symptoms, all of which contribute to the overall photo. Some examples of such factors encompass the range of inbound hyperlinks to a internet web web page and the authority of a such internet internet site.

There must be sufficient hobby inside the place of interest's number one keywords for it to be taken into consideration. The amount of people which is probably actively seeking out a few issue is your potential target market.

How lots an ad in this marketplace costs in step with click on on on will give you a top notch idea of ways intense the competition is. Advertisers are prepared to spend extra for added exposure if several of the most vital key phrases in your place of interest have a excessive CPC. It's high-quality information as it indicates there's cash to be obtained from promoting. But if the CPC is excessive, then might probably suggest that there is lots of opposition for that key-word and that it might be difficult to have your content material cloth seen. That is until you are inclined to spend extra.

You may also additionally furthermore estimate how hundreds cash you could make through analyzing the CPC and complexity of the important thing terms.

Remember that the motive of this studies is to determine whether or now not or no longer a satisfactory marketplace section is in reality really worth pursuing financially and to emerge as aware of any applicable opposition. After selecting a gap, you may dive into the meat of key-word studies: discovering key terms with low competition and notable volumes.

Investigate capability resources of site traffic.

Discover how plenty potential there can be for internet page visitors in a spot earlier than determining whether or not or no longer to invest time and power into it. Only with get right of entry to to a huge pool of capability clients can a sustainable, exceptional earnings be built.

Check out the net web sites and social media channels already dominating your ability market to look how they lure internet site visitors. Several enterprise and unfastened resources are available to you for this reason. Semrush, Ahrefs, and SimilarWeb are examples of such gear. Determine the relative contributions of paid advertising and marketing, herbal are in search of for, and social media to the internet site's total monthly website visitors. Take word of which social media systems are generating the first-class hobby on this particular region of hobby.

While some markets thrive on social media structures like Pinterest and Instagram, others depend nearly completely on backed or organic are searching out engine visitors. Start with the resource of compiling a listing of the maximum famous alternatives, after which examine their usefulness in mild of your regular marketing and marketing and advertising and marketing plan. Choose sub-markets that get website online visitors from channels that mesh on the aspect of your advertising campaign's reputation.

Learn how to differentiate your self from the competition.

To obtain achievement in any area, you want to have a one-of-a-type selling component.

So, accept as true with how you may differentiate your self from the opposition. And what is going to make your internet net web page or channel stand out and acquire success? More product earnings and commissions are possible with a nicely-described brand.

Strategizing a terrific point of view is important for each region of hobby. But it's in particular important for success in enormously aggressive regions. With maximum companion internet sites repeating huge and shallow content material cloth, you need to create cost to your site visitors thru a completely unique technique.

When deciding on your USP (specific promoting aspect), you want to make the most your abilities as a marketer. Do you accept as true with you studied you are proper at growing with easy mind for writing? Or, are you able to spice things up with a humorous video, a brilliant test, or a downloadable manual that no person else has? Can you prepare and display movement images pretty clearly? Do a few studies on the maximum well-known YouTube channels on your area of hobby and make a list of the subjects they may be doing well and wrong.

The trick is to check out of your opposition' successes and use those learnings for your content material method.

Spend a while developing a name, logo, or some different identifying photograph to your material so that you can assist readers understand it. In a market saturated with affiliate web sites that look and function further, that may be a sure way to face apart.

Where ought to I no longer bypass?

Specialized markets or contentious troubles that won't be proper for advertising and marketing

Blogging on arguable or in any other case unadvertisement-nice assignment subjects, at the side of the ones listed below, is some other on foot a weblog location you must keep away from:

- Politics

- The modern in titbits and showbiz

- Religion

- Subject depend regarding firearms and first rate lethal contraptions

- Alcohol-related content fabric

- Information related to smoking

- Contents of an Adult Nature

- Intimidation and violence

- Unsettling material

- Violence or extremely good probably risky behavior

- offensive language and imagery

- Drugs for amusing and cloth approximately drug use

You need to now not begin a weblog on those subjects due to the reality, first, there is already loads of content fabric obtainable on the undertaking, so that you won't be able to rise to the top of seek engine outcomes pages, and 2nd, this isn't always a mainly worthwhile location of hobby even if you grow to be an expert in the location and begin charging for advertising and advertising region in your net site on-line.

This technique that during 2022, it makes no experience to release a blog devoted to subjects like politics, gossip, sex, or adult material.

Chapter 4: Constructing My New Website

Definition of Landing Page

Clicks from an electronic mail, enterprise, or exquisite digital vacation spot might also moreover "land" human beings searching for merchandise/offerings on a dedicated net web web page. Landing pages are designed to collect leads in return for a present, which incorporates a discount voucher for a shop or a white paper entire of B2B insights. Landing pages are top notch from specific web pages while you consider that they're not frequently a part of a internet site's permanent navigation. Ads like this are designed to attain a nice demographic at a given time during a advertising and marketing marketing advertising and marketing campaign.

The the the front web page of a website frequently gives internet web site site visitors an advent to the employer. However, a landing web page is a big on line advertising and advertising channel for assisting with the finishing touch of a single, discrete venture within the consumer's adventure. Landing pages are very effective in changing net web site traffic into customers because of their recognition on a particular demographic.

Landing pages are first-class for on line marketing and advertising and marketing campaigns, but, QR codes on posted commercials also can be used to direct clients to the proper touchdown internet page. Conversion is the prevent intention of each advertising method, which makes landing pages an critical component.

After following a hyperlink from an ad, e mail, or every other online medium, the character "lands" on a dedicated internet net internet web page. Landing pages are an important part of any content approach for using extra visitors and growing sales.

Any traveler to your landing net web page need to be brought about to sign up for your mailing list or make a purchase. Your landing net web page has been successful if it effects in a conversion — defined due to the fact the character taking a few motion in your internet website.

Typically, a landing internet web page could excellent push one precise movement from the tourist, along with signing up the use of a unique shape confirmed at the net net page. Why?

This is because of the "paradox of desire," the concept that offering human beings with extra alternatives makes it more difficult for them to choose out one and skip on with their path of movement.

Consider that you are giving freely an eBook. However, your landing page furthermore includes calls to movement for readers to have a look at your weblog, buy a product, and study you on social media. The extra you inspire your consumers to do something else, the a good buy less possibly it's far that they'll download your new eBook.

Users also can get paralyzed by means of way of way of having too many alternatives, which may also moreover bring about nation of no interest. For this reason, it is quality to have one clean CTA in area of three or 4.

This is why a landing internet web page needs to be evaluated for maximum nice conversion optimization via having a easy visible hierarchy and value proposition.

There are fundamental sorts of touchdown pages.

Landing pages can be established to do one in each of things: either create leads or guide web site site visitors to the following level of the approach.

Lead technology landing internet web page

In the marketing international, touchdown pages designed mainly to gather lead statistics are mentioned variously as "lead gen" or "lead capture" pages. Meaning, that it assembles information approximately your clients.

In most instances, the selection to movement (CTA) on a lead seize page is probably within the form of a shape. Users are required to provide private records which encompass names, emails, and contact numbers in cross lower back for the services or products being supplied. More sure information, together with age stages or occupations, is also available upon request. In this method, you could have a look at up with leads and maintain their hobby in your business corporation developing.

Another feature is served by using using the use of this statistics. You can have a look at masses about your connections way to the data you got. If you recognize who your ideal consumer is, you can direct your advertising and marketing and advertising efforts in the direction of them. If you make investments coins in advertising, this could enhance your skip again on that funding.

In this method, the statistics gleaned from lead-generating websites can be used to sharpen and streamline your advertising efforts. You can motive simply those who are probable to transform, saving coins on classified ads that would otherwise be tested to those who aren't interested by what you're promoting.

Landing pages designed to generate leads are beneficial to corporations due to the reality they provide facts about their audience. Put a few idea into including one for your internet web page if lead nurturing is essential to you or in case you virtually need to look at extra about your internet site web site visitors.

Click-via landing pages

The number one functions of CTA landing pages are calls to motion in region of bureaucracy just like those visible on lead generation web websites. The button takes the individual to a cutting-edge net web web page in which they may do the desired pastime.

As an example, a button labeled "installation a demo" might also additionally lead the purchaser to a web page for making appointments, at the same time as a button classified "purchase X now" must link them to the proper checkout display.

To further trap and engage website on line website online site visitors, click on on on-thru landing pages regularly incorporate persuasive content cloth which includes product facts or customer testimonials further to the CTA button seen on e-commerce internet web sites and different web sites that prioritize producing on the spot purchases above gathering customer facts.

How to Create a Successful Website Home Page

1. Create a catchy, benefit-orientated headline.

At least 7 out of every 10 those who view your touchdown net web page may not stick spherical to convert. To hold a low leap price, it's far crucial that website on-line visitors right now see the advantages of visiting your web page. Your discover should proper now seize their interest and convey the significance of your touchdown internet page and offer.

2. Pick a picture that represents the deal nicely.

Yes, you need to encompass a photograph, and it ought to replicate who you're seeking to achieve. Your photo ought to display the traveller how they may revel in once they have received your offer. You need to generally cut up-check your selections (which we're able to undergo later) while you don't forget that certain photographs may also additionally perform better than others.

3. Create engaging textual content.

Don't positioned a tonne of attempt into developing a captivating headline and selecting the right photograph, excellent to fall quick on the subject of the duplicate so as to persuade readers to accomplish that. Your writing must be easy to apprehend and ought to lead the reader to take the favored motion. Using "you" and "you're" inside the textual content to make the reader feel like they're part of the communique is any other key to writing compelling content material. A more in-depth speak of reproduction advice follows.

4. Be excellent to position the lead form above the fold.

You do now not want your visitor to need to hunt and % approximately your landing internet internet page to find out the lead form and the provide you have positioned there. The term "above the fold" virtually refers back to the reality that the form is seen with out the need to scroll. Depending at the context, this will be a shape or a link to a form. Improve your shape's usability via making it scroll with the customer as they development down the net web page.

5. Include a incredible call to movement.

Among the severa elements that growth the threat of a conversion, the decision to movement (CTA) stands head and shoulders above the rest. For the choice-to-motion button to be seen, it must have a contrasting shade from the rest of the internet internet site on line. Use an motion verb like "placed up," "download," or "get it now" to inform readers exactly what you want them to do. Some tips for crafting effective CTAs observe.

6. Donate something of value.

Your touchdown net page need to be visible as a step alongside the route that outcomes on your very last provide. When a capability consumer fills out a form in your internet site, they're hoping to get some component in go back—your provide. It desires to be exciting sufficient for the traveler to need to head away their facts, and it wishes to be relevant on your organization. Consider your self a horseshoe service organisation.

An instance of a capability provide is a list like "10 Easy Ways to Size Your Horse's Hooves," with the closing reason of getting the result in buy horseshoes from you. In extraordinary terms, you may not attempt to trap them with an offer related to natural farming, considering it would lead them in an entirely specific direction. Further communicate at the splendor of gives will observe.

7. Don't problem asking for extra than you need.

You need to study as lots as you can approximately your lead, however how a bargain statistics you could get from them will range primarily based on their familiarity with you, in which they will be in the looking for method, and what sort of they agree with you. The lower the barrier to get right of entry to to your lead shape, the better. Having a touch's name and electronic mail address is all you want to begin nurturing a lead.

8. Got rid of the menus.

Your landing web web page's fine motive is to generate leads from website site traffic. Links to distinct internet web sites, or maybe one in every of a type sections of your web net web site, that compete with this one may be overlooked. To ensure that every reader's recognition is to your CTA, you ought to take away any competing content cloth.

nine. Make your web web page cell-exquisite.

Your touchdown pages, just like the relaxation of your website on-line, want to be mobile-excellent. Your form must be visible on cell devices always. Create a continuing individual revel in throughout all gadgets your internet website is considered on.

For this reason, you may employ many gadgets. For example, HubSpot's Marketing Hub Starter consists of a drag-and-drop landing web page builder that makes it smooth to design mobile-excellent touchdown pages and paperwork.

10. Search engine optimization.

Even despite the fact that you will be the usage of e-mail campaigns, social media, and one in all a kind sorts of marketing and advertising and marketing to get human beings on your landing net page, it's far no matter the fact that essential to make certain it is optimized for the important thing terms you need to rank for in paid search and organic searching for. Your landing net page wishes to be seen in are trying to find outcomes to your purpose key-word. When using backed advertisements to goal a certain term, that key-word need to additionally appear at the touchdown web web web page.

11. Use a thank you web net page to show your appreciation.

Once a prospect has stuffed out your shape, they need to be despatched to a "thank you" net web page. There are numerous drawbacks to truly showing a thank-you message on the equal net web page or skipping the thank-you in reality.

- There are 3 primary functions of a thank you web page:

- That fulfills your promise of a special deal (normally within the form of a direct download)

- By showing your new lead appreciation for their time and attention, you growth the probability that they may convert proper proper into a paying customer inside the future.

Start a Shop!

Even in case you've been considering setting up a web store for a while, getting began out may be daunting. This is in particular real in case you're not acquainted with the top notch info of the e-trade worldwide. Thankfully, the technologies available in recent times make launching a web company a terrific deal tons less of a trouble than ever in advance than.

Here are six clean steps to installing a store on the internet.

1. Determine Your Website's Address

You want a internet site address to do industrial enterprise on the Internet. This preference will serve as a instance of your commercial enterprise organisation, so select out it as it should be. A pinnacle commercial company name is probably memorable, easy to spell, and relevant in your business enterprise.

According to Total Shape's writer, Lianne Sanders, "it is recommended that you offer you with a one-of-a-type however actual sounding area name to ensure that you do now not appear suspect as fast as your online corporation turns into to be had on line." If you want to installation emblem reputation and keep your customers coming all over again, you need to make it as memorable and clean to recognize as possible.

2. Make Your Choice of an Online Store Software

There are numerous e-alternate systems handy, and no coding revel in is needed to apply them. Most of them have a few type of rate associated with every transaction, and a number of them have a month-to-month rate whilst others don't fee some thing in any respect. Sanders suggests going with a machine this is both green and pretty priced.

It's a no brainer, in line with Sanders, to make plenty of money however then surrender 1/2 of of it in club fees to the platform. "It's essential to enroll in the suitable issuer. One that gives everything you want on your online shop at an less expensive price."

three. You need to decide your USP.

You likely already understand the product(s) you need to marketplace. The subsequent problem you want to bear in mind is what makes your services or products precise from the competition.

Jeremy Harrison, creator of Hustle Life, a platform that enables people discover a element hustle like beginning an internet business, says, "I even have a look at the opposition and the way they do topics." "I determine out a way to enhance my standard performance. This is an vital step inside the machine and have to be taken earlier than starting any new mission."

four. Find Who You Want To Sell To

Your meant target audience is any other species that wishes to be defined. Knowing your goal market allows you to tailor your business enterprise organization's name, slogan, and promotional materials to a specific company of people.

According to Erma Williams, owner of The Pomade Shop, a shop of all-natural hair pomades, "discover your aim market via searching at the customers of related businesses." "Focus your advertising efforts on attractive to their pastimes. Locate the places they frequent, every on line and stale, and make it a thing to join them there. The subsequent step is to devise out how you can speak with this man or woman."

5. Do What You Can to Improve Your Site's Performance

It's no longer sufficient to area up a internet web site and assume that human beings will encounter it. It must be are looking for engine optimized to get human beings to go to it. Including applicable key terms in the object description is a great begin, but it need to no longer be the best approach you use.

Gilad Rom, CEO of Huan, a business company that distributes doggy monitoring tags, explains the organisation's advertising and marketing technique: "We deliberate to launch a blog focused on search engine optimization key phrases that furnished appropriate information and had the ability to rank excessive in are looking for engine consequences." This could possibly boom interest in our business enterprise employer and in the end cause more income.

After doing key-word studies, Rom installation a weekly publishing plan for his blog. Within four months, he provides, "we began to word traffic to our on-line maintain from our blog entries," which in the end prompted improved product earnings.

6. Educate the Public

Depending in your financial scenario, advertising and advertising and marketing is probably a high-priced organization. One of the co-owners of the mattress-in-a-field start-up Nolah Mattress, Stephen Light, recommends using the low-rate marketing and marketing opportunities offered thru social media whilst setting up your online business commercial enterprise agency.

The creator asserts that "social media advertising and marketing and marketing and advertising is a critical expenditure for agencies that choice to gather an internet presence," in particular human beings with online marketplaces. Gaining fanatics is an extended-time period strength of will, consequently the move returned on investment from social media marketing is greater than pay-consistent with-click.

Putting in extra strive now may additionally pay off inside the future. It's useless to invest coins on content material fabric distribution "after humans test your organization web page," provides Light. In one-of-a-type terms, "on the equal time as you publish, people see it proper away for gratis to you."

Launching a task in online shopping may be quite interesting. You can also lay the inspiration for a successful on-line store via enforcing a legitimate plan earlier than launching your net web web page.

WordPress vs. Shopify

Is Shopify or WordPress maximum ideal, and why? Many businesses marvel about this, and I need to provide an in-depth solution to this commonplace venture in this essay.

Keep reading for an intensive evaluation of Shopify vs Big change, similarly to a speak of the advantages and drawbacks of every platform for developing an internet keep.

After reading this, you want to have a much higher enjoy of which platform is most appropriate to satisfy the dreams of your agency (and what the remarkable options to each systems are).

Let's get subjects off with a fundamental question...

What is Shopify?

With Shopify, enterprise organization owners can create and control their e-exchange internet web sites.

It allows the sale of every bodily and digital devices and comes with a preference of pre-made layouts (referred to as "concern topics") that can be changed to wholesome the dreams of any precise commercial enterprise.

You can open a store on Shopify with out knowing a way to code, it is truely one of its important promoting elements.

While Shopify makes it clean to make minor changes for your on line maintain's look, advanced clients may additionally furthermore make greater great adjustments with statistics of HTML and CSS.

As a 'hosted' solution, Shopify handles the whole thing behind the scenes. Everything you want to set up and hold your business employer need to artwork 'out of the field,' which means you can not have to worry approximately things like shopping for an internet net hosting or putting in software program application.

(However, with the assist of applications, your Shopify keep may be tailor-made in your unique dreams; extra in this below).

Shopify is a "software program software as a service" (SaaS) platform, which means you do not certainly buy a license to use it but as an opportunity pay a subscription price to use it regularly.

Since Shopify is a web software, all you want to perform your on line hold is get entry to to the Internet and an internet browser. You can open a shop on Shopify with out facts the way to code, it's one in each of its maximum important selling elements.

While Shopify makes it clean to make minor adjustments to your on-line keep's look, superior clients may also make extra huge modifications with statistics of HTML and CSS.

As a 'hosted' solution, Shopify handles the whole thing behind the scenes. Everything you need to set up and keep your agency need to paintings 'out of the sector,' that means you could now not want to worry about things like purchasing a web internet website hosting or putting in software program software program.

(However, with the help of packages, your Shopify save can be tailor-made on your precise desires; more in this below).

Shopify is a "software program as a provider" (SaaS) platform, due to this you do no longer actually buy a license to apply it but as an opportunity pay a subscription rate to use it frequently.

Since Shopify is a web software program, all you want to feature your on-line keep is get admission to to the Internet and a web browser store from everywhere.

What is WordPress?

You may additionally moreover moreover pick out out amongst two super WordPress releases:

Hosted WordPress

Self-hosted WordPress

Hosted WordPress

Hosted WordPress (to be had at wordpress.Com) is a software program-as-a-issuer platform like Shopify.

In change for a subscription price (each month-to-month or every year), you may use their suite of device to create and manage a number one website, weblog, or online shop.

Here is a breakdown of what you have to assume to pay every month:

Monthly prices:

- Free — $0

- Personal — $7

- Premium — $14

- Business — $33

- eCommerce — $fifty nine

(If you pay for a 12 months earlier, the month-to-month charges for the Personal, Premium, Business and eCommerce plans are $4, $eight, $25, and $forty five, respectively.)

The 'Business' and 'eCommerce' plans are best in case you want to sell matters on-line thinking about that they permit for the installation of e-change plugins (and, within the case of the 'eCommerce' plan, effective greater e-alternate tools are also covered with the useful resource of way of default).

Self-hosted WordPress

Self-hosted Simply said WordPress is a piece of software program that can be received from wordpress.Org and then installation for your net server.

It's open supply, which means you could see and make changes to the underlying code at any time.

In reality, because of this WordPress-built websites may be changed in a massive shape of techniques; the platform is so versatile that it is able to be molded to in form the wishes of absolutely any net layout venture inside the hands of a expert internet site developer or with the help of suitable plugins.

Templates for the content fabric manipulate device WordPress. The platform's accessibility to loads of premade layouts is a main promoting factor.

WordPress set up is unfastened, however, there are ongoing charges like net internet hosting, vicinity call registration, or even improvement that can arise.

(I skip into in addition element on every of them in some time on this essay.)

Today, we may be contrasting the self-hosted model of WordPress (just like the ones positioned on WordPress.Com) with Shopify. The purpose of this text is to allow readers make an informed selection on whether or not or not or now not to go with Shopify, a hosted, "all-in-one" solution, or an open-supply platform that calls for additonal manual setup (WordPress).

This is also indicative of the fact that the majority of commercial WordPress e-trade internet net sites use the self-hosted model.

Chapter 5: Getting Customers

Sales Leads.

A profits lead is a person or corporation that has proven interest in shopping for your services or products. Whether it's a recommendation from a cutting-edge customer or a proper away reaction to a few shape of vending, the ones are the 2 maximum common resources of leads. Typically, a organisation's marketing organization may be in rate of finding new possibilities.

The sales workforce is usually chargeable for following up on leads and making earnings. For instance, sooner or later of a exchange trustworthy geared in the direction of a superb corporation, a vendor or channel accomplice within the facts technology quarter may promote it its wares inside the hopes of attracting interested, probable licensed customers. Any time a functionality purchaser expresses hobby in getting to know more about your business enterprise, you've got a new lead.

There is not any huge for the information that constitutes a income lead. Potential patron information might be as clean as a name and electronic mail cope with, or it may encompass a better profile of the customer, which includes the customer's function in her agency and when they assume to make a buy. The remarkable of a company's lead generation and the way it handles leads can also have a prime impact at the organization's bottom line. To gain this aim, most businesses try and build inexperienced techniques for lead technology, qualifying, and transport.

Sales lead generation assets

Sales lead introduction is step one inside the earnings leads acquisition process. As part of the advertising system, lead turbines are used to create ability clients' interest. The most vital method of producing new leads is to ask satisfied customers to spread the word. However, businesses that want a speedy earnings boom often use one in every of a kind lead creation strategies. For instance, they'll pay a lead-producing commercial enterprise organization to provide them with a listing of functionality customers. Direct advertising and marketing takes many forms, and mailing lists, e-mail lists, and call lists are all tools that may be carried out to attain capability clients.

Businesses can also create leads through internet website hosting or attending B2B sports. Trade exhibitions, on-line webinars, and lunch-and-studies seminars are all examples of event marketing efforts. With the advent of digital advertising and marketing came a plethora of new strategies to generate leads. Digital advertising and marketing techniques, alongside facet inbound marketing, purpose to draw earnings leads the usage of employer-generated net content fabric in place of through traditional, direct advertising strategies. Blog articles, films, infographics, and white papers are all particular examples of cloth that can be used for inbound advertising and advertising and advertising and marketing. Organizations can also market it their products and services with the beneficial resource of the usage of a Material advertising and marketing and marketing and marketing method once they produce and disseminate inbound marketing and advertising and marketing content material.

In addition to traditional net marketing and marketing channels, inbound techniques increasingly more use mobile and social media channels.

Sales lead control manner

If your lead era efforts are fruitful, you could have profits leads of diverse characteristics and urgency to take a look at up on. A employer may additionally additionally increase the charge of its leads through imposing a lead manage method, moreover referred to as lead-to-income control, which includes techniques and equipment for producing, coping with, and delivering results in salespeople.

The cause of income leads control is to fill a employer's profits funnel with certified possibilities. Lead scoring, or the assessment and rating of leads based on wherein the feasible purchaser sits within the shopping for funnel or profits funnel, is normally the purview of the marketing department. A patron's journey via the earnings funnel (occasionally known as the customer's journey or profits cycle) starts offevolved at the equal time as they may be first made aware of a services or products and ends with a buy.

Types of leads

The marketing and advertising group usually assigns a rating to each lead at a few diploma within the common purchaser's journey, whether or now not it's miles inside the shape of factors or a temperature scale (therefore the names "cold" and "heat" leads). In addition to being represented in terms of lead scoring, lead qualification is every other not unusual manner of describing leads.

There are many wonderful categories of sales leads, every of that's said via one of the following phrases:

-     Suspects: Visitors to a supplier's net site looking for large facts about a product or service on the top of the buying funnel are frequently called suspects. The intention of lead nurturing is to expand possibilities farther down the earnings funnel inside the path of a completely final transaction. Lead nurturing is preserving in touch with functionality clients and presenting them with applicable information as they are in search of it.

-     Cold, warm, and warm leads: Leads can be categorised as cold, warmness, or warm through the use of entrepreneurs and salespeople, respectively, based totally on the amount of hobby or preparedness of the potential patron to make a buy. A warm lead is a functionality client who has confirmed an urgent need in your carrier, has supplied a price variety and has set a timeline for while you could start offering that service. In assessment, a "warmth lead" can also advocate a capability client's interest in a product however now not but have the belongings to decide to a buy. The BANT (rate range, authority, want, time body) technique is used by sure entrepreneurs and salespeople to classify leads as cold, heat, or heat.

-       Market-qualified lead: Leads can be labeled as bloodless, warmth, or heat by entrepreneurs and salespeople, respectively, based totally totally mostly on the amount of hobby or preparedness of the capability client to make a purchase. A heat lead is a ability purchaser who has proven an urgent want to your service, has provided a fee variety and has set a timeline for even as you may start imparting that issuer. In evaluation, a "heat lead" may additionally additionally additionally endorse a capacity client's interest in a product but no longer however have the property to commit to a buy. The BANT (rate range, authority, want, time body) technique is used by superb entrepreneurs and salespeople to classify leads as bloodless, heat, or heat.

- Sales-licensed lead: A SQL right now indicates their purpose to shop for, making them a capacity earnings prospect. The advertising and advertising and marketing and advertising and advertising and marketing branch then palms over the SQL to the earnings department. Product organizations within the IT channel may additionally distribute certified leads they produce to channel partners like fee-brought resellers (VAR).

Using Influencers to Create Free Leads

Market valuations for influencer advertising and marketing are projected to boom from $6.5 billion in 2019 to $thirteen.Eight billion in 2021. Brand reputation, net internet site online visits, best leads, and extra sales may also furthermore all end result from data the manner to find out and collaborate with the right influencers.

Finding the proper internet influencers to help sell your contest or new product release may be a undertaking. Most individuals lose up after they ask themselves, "How inside the worldwide can I get Beyonce or Kylie Jenner to present me a shoutout?"

Luckily, promoting your business enterprise company does not need paying quite a few cash to a well-known celebrity. Micro-influencers can be observed in any area, and they're generally open to operating with others on a smaller scale. Utilize those guidelines as a starting point in your hunt for influencers to collaborate with. These guidelines will lead you to the influencers who may be maximum beneficial in kicking off your advertising and marketing advertising marketing campaign.

1. Recognize Your Desired Outcomes

The first step in choosing influential human beings is to come to be privy to and description those targets. To what amount do you require a benefactor of a first-rate kind? What precisely is it that you need them to perform for you? With nicely-defined objectives in thoughts, you will be able to 0 in at the agencies, profiles, and people maximum possibly to beneficial useful resource you in connecting together collectively with your intention demographic and generating the results you need.

The first step in developing an effective influencer advertising method is to decide what you want to achieve. Here are some possible objectives for your advertising and marketing and marketing:

1. Gaining an Audience

2. Exposure to the Brand

3. Product reputation

four. Profits from dedicated customers

5. Link-building for Customer Involvement and Website Visits

Having nicely-described key goals makes it much less complicated to assess influencer connections and determine whether or not or now not they'll contribute to the desired effects.

Discover Key Opinion Leaders in Your Sector

After choosing a direction of motion, it is time to start searching out influential people for your discipline. But how do you bypass about tracking out the right influencers in your logo? You can also locate an business enterprise influencer thru manner of following the ones 3 easy steps:

A. Use a Contest to Determine Who to Follow

To sell your business agency without being too "salesy," try protective a competition. They are a completely unique technique to boosting client involvement and reputation of your corporation with out resorting to overt marketing and advertising. They make interacting along side your brand thrilling and appealing for the patron. Applications like KickoffLabs may be used to find the best influencers in your corporation.

Each lead in a KickoffLabs contest is given a rating based totally on how actively they participated. The greater humans interact in conjunction with your brand (through referrals, social media following, content cloth sharing, and so on.), the more elements they get. Anyone with a immoderate sufficient issue general merits to have nearer ties mounted with them.

Hold a opposition as a part of the marketing and marketing campaign to recognize the essential thing opinion leaders. You can also additionally, for instance, choose to prioritize candidates who can offer more than or three references. You need to search for those who have spent greater than a couple of minutes getting to know approximately your brand or sharing it with others. The pinnacle 5-10% of respondents are the micro-influencers you have got formerly installation relationships with.

B. Evaluate the Audiences of Your Rivals

Look for micro-influencers which are already running with or have worked with corporations which is probably much like yours to benefit the notable endorsements to your product. People in such positions of strength are more likely to spread the phrase approximately your organisation via articles and social media posts. The influencers that routinely put up articles approximately your competition may be located with the aid of manner of using attempting to find hashtags regarding your region on social media. Then, contact them in an try to negotiate a compromise.

You may additionally check credible micro-influencers to help marketplace your corporation through finding out who your closest competition are following or the images they've got tagged on their feed. Most possibly, your competition have already tagged or are following micro-influencers who sell them.

C. Tool Up

It is feasible to locate the right influencers in your subsequent advertising and marketing marketing campaign at the identical time as no longer having to spend time doing it manually if you use the proper gear. You may also moreover find pinnacle social media influencers, publishers, and bloggers, examine them and phone them with the use of the ones gadget.

Scrunch: All the equipment, from discovery to analytics, for strolling a achievement influencer advertising campaigns are protected on this freemium offering. Using its advanced filtering system, you can find the influencers who're the exceptional fit on your campaigns.

Heepsy: More than 11 million influencers across Instagram, TikTok, and YouTube are at your fingertips with this on hand app.

Modash: As one of the leading influencer databases, it permits organizations find out the maximum applicable influencers for his or her marketing and advertising and marketing campaigns. In addition, the software program allows agencies to preserve based totally databases of artists.

Buzzsumo: Using this app, you can find out a number of Instagram's and Twitter's most influential clients.

inBeat: There isn't any higher region to look than inBeat for a unsolicited mail-checked database of influential people. The achievement of this tool is based totally on metrics and seed key phrases. Keywords, hashtags, or maybe your competitors' names can be implemented in inBeat that will help you locate influential humans to have a look at.

Klear: You can also use this app to look for influencers in a incredible vicinity or internal a specific situation. With its advanced gear, you could goal unique subsets of your aim marketplace primarily based totally on their demographics, interests, and in which they live.

Followerwonk: You can find out an appropriate logo ambassadors and expand your targeted following with the help of this to be had device. Using Followewonk, you could find out Twitter influencers and research extra approximately their followers to determine whether they may be an exquisite in shape for your employer.

Social Studies: If you are trying to community with influential human beings in your industry, you have got come to the right area.

Any company can find out the nice net influencer. The hassle is to choose an influencer that meets your organisation's necessities. Using the ones techniques, you may find out the perfect influencer on your organization with absolute fact.

The aforementioned tool is not exhaustive. One of the goals is to pick out influential humans who have 10,000 or fewer lovers.

Use Your Blog to Get Free Leads

Create a Lead Generation Machine with These Blogging Strategies

Curious about the precise strategies utilized by a success bloggers to attract new readers and make profits? What follows is a condensed model of the strategies advocated to us through our experts:

- Make compelling lead magnets.

- Put your spin on topics whilst you write.

- Make statistics that others will discover beneficial.

- Make sure you have got were given content material fabric for each step of the income device.

- Provide limited access to pinnacle elegance content material cloth Collaborate with profits to better apprehend your goal demographic

- Upsell present day content material cloth material

- If you'll employ a key-phrase, do no longer limit yourself too much.

- Lead technology is lots much less hard with a speak widget.

- Introduce a "whats up" bar to your website online and trap pick out-ins

- Include a name to movement in all your writing (CTA)

- Incorporate person-generated fabric

- Be aware about the motivations underlying your goal market's searches.

- Find the ideal key terms.

-      Include a touch form on your blog articles.

-      Promote the articles you have got written on your blog on numerous social networks.

-      Conduct polls and provide stuff away.

-      To increase visitors on your weblog, you might use the question-and-answer internet web page Quora.

-      Make a aid that covers the whole lot and market it it widely.

-      Optimize your blog with properly placed pop-ups.

-      Increase your internet site's website online site visitors thru manner of which incorporates retargeting tags and special content material material upgrades.

Getting Free Sales Leads From Social Media

Five-fifty-five percentage of all net customers now spend time every day on social networks. The widespread volumes of facts they provide to the systems each day are made feasible through way of their usage of it. You may also additionally furthermore use this records to generate leads through social media. To positioned it some other manner, it gives advertisers a right away line to their supposed clients.

The truth is that there are a few motives for this:

- Competitiveness has extended in the concern of search engine optimization. Each next update extensively will boom the problem. Some internet web sites that used to rank with out hassle all at once have a much more tough time doing so. Many of those internet websites are trying to find digital advertising and marketing and advertising techniques that could help them compete.

- Spending a large amount of money on search engine optimization is vital even for a brand-new internet site.

- It's high-priced. In evaluation to social media, wherein the fee in keeping with conversion is $1, advertising through search engines like google may cost a little as a bargain as $4 or $5.

Chapter 6: Ideas For Efficient

Interaction

Techniques for Effective Interaction

Strong strains of conversation are the bedrock of each a achievement employer. If you want to assemble lasting connections and whole important duties, you and your coworkers need to have the ability to talk properly with each exceptional at work. This is particularly right whilst running with freelancers and a long way off organizations.

Communicating with others not best makes you enjoy appropriate, however it additionally has tangible results. Misunderstandings, disappointments, and angry customers are all possible effects of communication troubles.

Here at Up stack, we've give you 10 clean recommendations based totally at the interest that we perform each day to permit you to cope with the ones issues and beautify your verbal exchange and teamwork.

1. Learn to concentrate

People frequently absolutely want to experience like they will be being heard. It's hard to discover common ground if neither party is listening to the other's terms. Don't daydream, plan your subsequent retort, or lessen the alternative character in mid-sentence; as a substitute, take note of what they'll be pronouncing.

2. Check your frame language

Be approachable and display openness in your frame language at meetings, whether or not they're in man or woman or digital. This consists of preserving fingers at your factors, eyes dealing with ahead, and table/pen play to a minimal. The most crucial piece of recommendation is to make and maintain eye touch with the alternative person.

three. Double test earlier than hitting the deliver button

Grammar and spellcheckers store masses of time, however they may be not wonderful. Verify which you have expressed yourself absolutely with the aid of the use of way of reading what you have got had been given written aloud.

four. Keep it brief and particular

If you need someone to virtually get what you are pronouncing to them, whether or not verbally or in writing, exercising being concise however as unique as possible. Neither too little nor too much facts is right. There must be no evasions.

five. Write it down!

To one's detriment, the thoughts plays recommendations on memory from time to time. It's an notable idea to write down notes in case you're having a conversation or attending a meeting with some one-of-a-kind character. After the assembly, it is easy to send a follow-up electronic mail summarising the important thing points noted, making sure that everyone turn out to be on the equal net web page.

6. Stop. Think. Talk.

Don't actually blurt out the whole lot that involves thoughts. Be quiet for a 2nd before you open your mouth. It's crucial to pause for a minute and consider the way you want your message to encounter. The range of socially uncomfortable or embarrassing conditions you could keep away from is huge.

7. Make your workflow apparent

Make positive all people is at the equal web page about a venture by way of way of using the usage of a undertaking manipulate tool like Asana, Trello, or Excel Sheets. Get rid of the pressure of not knowing where you're in a assignment via way of the use of a mission monitoring tool.

eight. Sharing is being concerned

Hiding facts that might benefit the collective isn't surely egocentric but moreover risky to the organization as an entire. If you've got had been given get entry to to a hyperlink, a newsfeed, or some problem else that could spur boom, you could not only advantage from it, however you may rapid emerge as a depended on useful resource and the "glue" that holds businesses collectively.

9. Equality for all people

Be respectful to others and keep away from patronizing them the least bit prices. When each person in a group is dealt with similarly, it conveys a revel in of safety and reliability.

10. Smile and maintain a awesome mindset

If you answer the mobile cellphone with a smile and an splendid thoughts-set, you could get a similarly upbeat response. Instead of slowing down productivity and making human beings grumpy, a glad mind-set might likely speed subjects up. If you need your industrial employer and your personnel to thrive, you need to ensure you're speakme correctly with each one-of-a-kind.

Tips for Dealing with an Irate or Reluctant Customer

Customers' crossed palms, heaved sighs, and short solutions are all signs that they are losing interest in what you are announcing, and that your possibilities of keeping their organisation are diminishing rapidly.

Often, clients who're hard or perhaps unfavourable are not venting their dissatisfaction with you. Situations and internal cues each have a position in eliciting the ones feelings. Instead of dropping a patron due to a false impression, located your exquisite interpersonal abilities to use with the aid of reading the state of affairs correctly and the usage of the ones 8 highbrow suggestions for managing difficult clients.

1. Practice reflective listening.

Do the words "I apprehend" help you while you're disenchanted? Not in my opinion. The patron will no longer feel better after paying attention to the form of favored comment. Consider the subsequent instance:

Disappointed purchaser: "We have a outstanding finances and also you aren't organized to present us a reduction."

Manager of Customer Success: "I get it, however..."

As you may see, the alternate up pinnacle isn't always doing well.

Instead, educate yourself to pay interest thoughtfully. One of the keys to powerful reflective listening is studying to take a look at the speaker's intentions via their phrases and frame language. After taking inventory of the situation, you might solution through echoing the customer's sentiments.

Example of schooling reflective listening:

Disappointed purchaser: "We have a first rate fee variety and also you aren't prepared to give us a reduction."

Sales and Marketing Manager: "So, I take it that our expenses are a turnoff for you. You have a restrained price range, and alas, my bargain may not assist you out. So, you accept as true with it, right?"

If you've got were given grasped the essence of their this means that, you could proceed. If no longer, then you definitely should respond, "Tell me greater so I also can higher apprehend." Don't offer the have an effect on that you can alternate the situation thru the use of pronouncing you may. Right now, your aim need to be to make the consumer experience that they're essential to you.

2. Consider their effect heuristic.

To make short judgments approximately human beings, places, and activities, the have an impact on heuristic can be used as a intellectual shortcut. It explains why remarkable people have specific views and values whilst making similar options and exams.

There is little weight given to tough records thru approach people in those conditions. In its region, we usually will be inclined to run the selection or scenario through our private inner "software" and form our conclusions based on what we already recognize. A person's have an effect on heuristic may be very man or woman and based totally mostly on their particular set of lifestyles events.

A continual client must likely "It's not usually useful to say such things as, "You've already acquired an annual club for this advertising and advertising software. What's the lure?" after which drag out the onboarding technique with rescheduling and endless due diligence. Can we hold in the mean time?"

Your patron might also had been duped into signing a one-12 months agreement with a enterprise that fell short in their expectations. Customers' perceptions of you have got got been fashioned via manner of their experience.

Example of the have an impact on heuristic:

To get to the lowest of their concerns, ask clarifying questions. Using the following questions, you may placed your consumer comfortable even as additionally mastering greater approximately why they may be hesitant to preserve:

"Please supply an motive for it to me; I need to research. Elucidate your skepticism's origins for me."

The question, "What can I do to calm your nerves?"

I want to recognise what I can do to make you feel consistent enough to take the following step.

The respondent's cognizance shifts from you being untrustworthy to the sources they need to progress because of your queries.

three. Tap into the amateur's thoughts.

The novice's thoughts frequently referred to as the zen thoughts, is the mentality of treating every situation as in case you have been encountering it for the primary time. By adopting this mind-set, you could technique each interplay with the patron with out making assumptions approximately them or their characteristic.

It teaches you to allow cross of the "shoulds" that plague your life. Insights which incorporates, "The customer want to have observed out they wouldn't have price range until next location" are examples of such bothersome mind.

The customer became warned in an electronic mail however did now not check it earlier than the sale ended.

That I may be to be had every week for consultations changed into an unrealistic expectation on the part of the consumer.

When you operate "shoulds," you right now located yourself at the protective, which undermines the effectiveness of the talk.

The zen thoughts-set requires giving up the want to understand everything. You may additionally moreover apprehend loads about your organisation's offerings and feature even honed your customer service skills, but there may be a terrific hazard you do now not comprehend a good deal approximately the specifics of this customer's feature or the prevailing communicate.

Example of tapping into the novice's thoughts:

Instead of saying things like, "You cautioned me you desired to growth your inbound lead technology by means of manner of way of 20 percent with the useful useful resource of the prevent of this month and those delays may not make this possible," attempt drawing near every communique with a sense of marvel and interest, as in case you had been taking note of some issue for the primary time. Don't count on the patron is satisfied, positioned apart your mind on what they must have finished, and word each interaction as a clean hassle to be solved.

You may additionally moreover strive putting forward, "It now appears not going that we're able in an effort to generate enough incoming leads with the useful resource of our reduce-off date. But permit's take a look at out our options and see if we are able to acquire our desires." This approach acknowledges the problem handy but proper away gets to artwork resolving it.

four. Let skip of fear.

Many of our sports activities activities are endorsed through our worry of the possible consequences. The commonplace human response to dread is to try to exert dominion over the state of affairs. There is a reluctance to confront a disturbing client for worry of harming the connection with that client. We fear that if a client complains approximately our turnaround time or our fees, we might not be capable of make subjects right.

Get rid of the perception that everything is damaged. It is not your obligation to fast deliver a solution whilst assembly with a tough consumer; rather, it is your duty to listen, analyze, and decide the subsequent steps.

Example of letting cross of fear:

Instead of apologizing, offering a half of of of-hearted answer, or looking to validate the opposite man or woman's emotions, strive pronouncing, "That X befell in any respect is a disgrace. I apprehend the impact that is having in your employer and I thank you in your records even as I attempt to find out a answer."

5. "Chunk" the trouble.

The term "chunking" refers back to the exercising of dividing a large trouble into multiple smaller ones. Pieces like this are more possible, and that they inspire us to begin working at the trouble. Many humans use chunking as a time manage device or to useful resource with complex troubles.

Example of "chunking" the problem:

Is it not unusual for a consumer to make excuses about why they cannot create an account and begin making use of your product? Please ask them that will help you put together the ultimate duties at your subsequent assembly. When your customer sees the remaining artwork damaged down into attainable chunks, they may have a miles less complex time preserving tune of what needs to be finished.

6. Remember that anger is herbal.

Have you ever tossed out a price or time determination and visible the client increase disillusioned, even furious, at how lots it prices or how extended it might take? Perhaps you have got were given enjoy at the possibility factor. What a customer is inclined to pay to your new and advanced items receives you indignant, mainly if it's far plenty lots less than you were awaiting.

According to the Recalibration Theory of Anger, human beings' capability to experience anger is hardwired. In a nutshell, rage is clearly our evolved technique of haggling. To result in our "opponent" to rate what we have got got at a extra rate, we furrow our brows, squeeze our lips together, and flare in a single nostril.

Example of the use of anger to good buy with a purchaser:

Stay calm and chorus from protecting your self in competition to an irate customer. Instead, try to see it from their perspective; they may be simplest in search of to regain manipulate after feeling devalued.

Listen for your disenchanted clients however do not take it in my view. Keep your cool and be aware of what the customer is announcing. When you've got were given mounted that you've grasped the gravity in their dilemma, it is appropriate to specific gratitude for their candor and promise to return once more once more to them with a treatment.

If a client is already dissatisfied, it is no longer likely that some element will calm them down. Give them time to loosen up, speak in your manager approximately the way to address the trouble, after which take the recommendation underneath to make subjects better.

7. Keep calm and preserve on.

In business agency, conflicts are inevitable; the manner you reply to criticism determines the lengthy-time period health of your clients.

The antique announcing, "The purchaser is constantly right," is greater relevant than ever. Dropping to a patron's negative level is a unstable pass with a long manner higher stakes if you inquire from me.

Negative exposure for your self and your agency can also quit give up result from treating people rudely, so shielding your reputation is usually critical.

Keep in mind that others are probable to mirror the feelings you deliver. Do not expect a warmth and compassionate response from someone to whom you've got been unfavorable and angry.

Example of ultimate calm:

The following are some techniques for coping with an emotionally charged scenario:

Don't become too flustered, but hold your tone businesslike and competitive.

Please do not get private or thing palms.

Nothing proper ever got here from saying or writing some thing that can be used inside the route of you.

Disputes need to be settled face-to-face or over the cellphone. When it entails solving conflicts, electronic mail is inefficient.

Dan Tyre, the Director of Sales at HubSpot and a 30-one year income veteran, says, "If you are like maximum human beings, you can supply in on your feelings. Great people see probabilities like the ones and take advantage of them. Lean in, try to positioned your self in [they're] footwear, pay attention cautiously, and display a few compassion."

eight. Use your useful resource assets.

- The customer support gadget are what my colleague Clint Fontanella calls "guns on your armory." You may additionally furthermore make use of these techniques in the course of a mobile phone touch, online chat, or face-to-face meeting with a difficult consumer.

- In any event, right proper here are severa gear that your salespeople want to end up fluent in, but they must most effective be applied as desired:

- Putting a patron on wait as a negotiating tactic or to calm them down.

- How to provide an reason behind a complex solution by means of way of the use of the use of show sharing or recording troubleshooting strategies.

- Having the self belief for your technique to invite a coworker for affirmation. (This may additionally additionally help you connect with a skeptical patron and win them round in your issue of view.)

Example of the use of your sources:

Let's preserve in thoughts taken into consideration one in all your maximum committed clients earrings in with a totally famous complaint, but they insist it's far a complex trouble. While you are displaying them the tested approach, they argue that they have got already finished the whole lot you said they should. They are getting angry due to the fact they receive as actual with you don't consider that they have got done your commands.

The time to use a strategic maintain couldn't be better than proper now. Inform the patron which you might want to research this depend variety further to make sure that their products or services is functioning usually. You can also assure them which you are checking for problems and solving them thru pronouncing that you are taking walks exams, consulting a colleague, or doing diagnostics.

Wait a minute or in silence, then pass decrease again on the street and suggest that you and the client strive troubleshooting once more. This locations you in a win-win characteristic because of the fact you will each capture the purchaser's mistake or you may find out the oddity without making the client enjoy like they will be needlessly retracing their steps.

All of those essential moves have one issue in commonplace even as managing disillusioned customers: listening to them. To better cope with disillusioned customers, it's miles crucial to pay interest their comments.

Chapter 7: Living A Life That Is Rich In

Joy, Success, And Fulfilment.

How To Be a Happy And Prosperous Business Owner

There are masses of books approximately commercial enterprise agency and existence success. Tomorrow, every other thousand articles can be posted at the trouble. With happiness being this form of significant trouble, it could be tough to distill it proper right down to a easy list that without a doubt everybody can take a look at and use.

You'll find out comparable troubles for the duration of loads of books, articles, and even recollections and memories. Many dad and mom bear in mind but in no way attempt to perform the ones simple requirements. You'll pay attention approximately beliefs and options absolutely everyone preference we may need to understand. Here are 10 topics you may discover in the achievement tales of agency corporation (and lifestyles) leaders. How many do you have got?

1. Be Fearless

Why is a enterprise employer success so hard? The first-rate hassle is overcoming the concern of beginning a business enterprise. Most people daydream of beginning a enterprise organisation at the same time as strolling humdrum jobs. They never depart the comfort of a sales because of the truth they're terrified of the unknown. Learn to cope with your anxieties to stand out from the organisation. Not unaided on the same time as I resigned from my art work to start my organization, I modified into earning two times my eight-hour profits. I feared failing.

If you need to attain corporation, you want to hold going despite the fact that topics come to be difficult. It takes courage to face your anxieties and set up a agency, however the real exams of a fearless entrepreneur can be ongoing: from making small communicate at a networking event to last a big settlement to decreasing connections with a companion who is hurting the project to seeing the enterprise collapse (it occurred to Henry Ford times in advance than he invented the assembly line). A loss of fear permits someone to strive and fail severa times earlier than ultimately succeeding.

2. Understand Finance

It's common understanding that the concept for a famous brand regularly started out in someone's home basement or garage. It is regularly believed that a a success entrepreneur is one that rose from humble beginnings. Most a hit organizations require cash to obtain success. You do now not need masses of cash to begin started, but you need to recognize how finance works and the manner to make use of your coins to amplify.

Robert Kiyosaki taught the world the want of monetary literacy for entrepreneurs. Those that live profits to profits have automobile and loan payments, credit score cards, and one-of-a-kind commitments. Financially savvy human beings recognize the need of gathering property as an alternative. Once your asset column is excessive best, you can invest to generate extra cash. Successful marketers understand a manner to placed money to work.

3. Grow As A Leader

When you overcome your anxieties and installation a business enterprise, you turn out to be a leader. Your success is primarily based upon on the way you help others discover theirs, as we are able to see. Many parents understand a fulfillment organizations like a famous quarterback or sizable receiver. These people constantly lead a crew to victory. You should be a pacesetter to influence humans to sign up for your undertaking, recall what you train, or purchase your services or products.

Just due to the fact you require control abilties does no longer suggest you need to be the CEO or "in control" When Google started out out to extend, its engineers-grew to grow to be-CEOs employed Eric Schmidt to move the agency. It takes enchantment and the capability to hold a message to encourage enthusiasts to comply with a leader. A splendid soldier can command infantrymen on the field, but not a conflict. Super product designers can be terrible salespeople. A sturdy leader is aware of their strengths and weaknesses and is privy to who to area and in which to guarantee their commercial enterprise corporation's success.

4. Use Your Leverage

One of the biggest obstacles an entrepreneur has is understanding what to do with opportunities. People entering a commercial enterprise employer want to apprehend leverage, and additionally it requires a particular form of brainpower to expect "beyond the sector" to discover price in a modern connection or setting. Natives who are afraid to move away their employment don't know how to utilize their property and connections. A successful entrepreneur creates income and opportunities every day.

"When existence gives you lemons, create lemonade" is an terrific instance of commercial corporation leverage. Many make and consume lemonade. A real entrepreneur sells lemonade to others without lemons and uses the income to shop for more lemons or begin a few other enterprise. Donald Trump, a contentious politician, is a surely nice instance of an entrepreneur who applied power to acquire key real property or negotiate worthwhile commercial enterprise partnerships. In his e-book "The Art of the Deal," he demonstrates that the usage of leverage may additionally help you acquire your dreams.

five. Acquire Partners

To "pass the chains" in commercial enterprise, you want leaders. To be a remarkable leader, you want a group that believes in the mission. A notable group of partners is essential to every thriving organisation. Numerous start by myself and placed on many roles, but a business organisation can great growth thus far with one supply of strength, creativity, and sweat equity.

A real "enterprise agency proprietor" does not need to be worried in day by day operations for the corporation to achieve achievement. "The E-Myth," tells what number of humans strive (and fail) to begin their very own enterprise. Instead, you ought to inspire human beings to apply their competencies as a group for the agency's sake. This entails expertise who to quake arms with, a manner to form deliberate relationships, and the way to utilize have an effect on to have interaction people on your agency. Once you obtain fulfillment, it is going to be even higher to percentage it with folks that aided you.

6. Having the Right Attitude

We've explored several vital business mind, but how do you outline fulfillment? Is it cash, income, or the surroundings you affect? Real commercial enterprise achievement most effective counts if it translates to private achievement, and that begins offevolved offevolved with the excellent mindset. Rich folks that despise their lives are overlooked.

The story of Ebeneezer Scrooge, a stingy vintage guy who with the aid of way of a few technique manages to live depressing regardless of his wealth, is broadly recognized.

To live a satisfied and sizable existence, you have to decide what's essential and set up ethics approximately what you could do each days to gather that global. Diverse entrepreneurs crave economic freedom. What do wealthy human beings do with their money? Those who expect having cash method buying extra "subjects" to feel superior will in no way gain success. Entrepreneurs that focus on developing riches to assist others and resolve issues have an appropriate mentality to be glad and respected by using manner of their colleagues and partners; they exemplify "fulfillment."

7. Showing Gratitude

Every day, our worldwide changes at a charge we can all understand. In the beyond 30-50 years, generation has changed how we hook up with buddies, loved ones, and agency companions worldwide. Those who've grown up on this technological age generally generally tend to take it all without any consideration, forgetting to "scent the flora" and recognize the truth that they may be lucky to have such quite a few present day conveniences, which include the capability to show on their lighting fixtures and strain themselves to artwork.

Those who take time to apprehend their environment generally have a tendency to be a success professionally and in my view. They famend the barista's efforts in making their morning espresso, starting doors, and paying hobby. When walking a commercial enterprise enterprise, it is crucial to don't forget the people, locations, and subjects that carried out a function to your achievement. Think about Louis CK's "chair within the sky" shaggy dog tale the following time you're on a plane and take into account to be thankful for the stunning topics in existence.

eight. Staying Healthy

Why may you danger your health for cash and success? What particular is business company ardour in case you won't see it thru? Too many human beings get stuck up in life and do no longer don't forget the harm they inflict on their our bodies. As entrepreneurs, lunch breaks are so busy that we consume speedy meals to meet our appetites. I consume fast.

Sometimes we burn the candle at every ends, the use of the day's anxiety as an excuse to drink and use capsules. Do we diploma fulfillment with the aid of idolizing superstars who died younger? Our fixation with foreign places cash and material items makes us insatiable and tense approximately ourselves and others. Without fitness, we can not succeed. A chief must be sturdy, and we are no longer quality talking about a slim body or muscle mass - your mind ought to be wholesome to go through through the day and enjoy achievement.

nine. Keeping the Right Friends

We have said the importance of not trying to find to construct your enterprise corporation on my own. The identical is actual for your well-being and fulfillment. Without high-quality human beings, what's the point in conducting anything? No one desires to be known as "Bruce Wayne," the town quack whose own family constantly leaves him an area on the desk.

Social human beings need a lifestyles slight of labor. Your friends will excessive-5 you with every achievement and select you up after every setback. Make positive they proportion your mindset, are thankful, and are an wonderful have an effect on. Negative-energy eaters may moreover supply down the entire domestic.

10. The Importance of Family

We've mentioned what drives us to emerge as commercial enterprise employer proprietors and the manner to installation large desires. Most start off needing cash or strength. These sports are frequently non-public and egocentric, but someone wanting real fulfillment will accomplish that to percent with their friends and own family.

We've noted what drives us to turn out to be organization proprietors and a manner to set up substantial desires. We may not all have youngsters or soulmates. Success is greater than cash or electricity, however. Having a incredible effect on loved ones and the those who will keep on your name is the last degree of achievement.

Chapter 8: Managing Your Orders

(Workload)

Managing your order float is an essential detail of handling your purchaser's satisfaction. This is as it enables you be on pinnacle of factors and not permit any ball drop. In this bankruptcy, we spotlight some techniques if you need to govern your workflow and make certain you do not skip over any possibilities.

Managing your workload allows you moreover may additionally optimize your conversation together with your client.

6.1   How to successfully music and manage workflow

To efficaciously music and manage your workflow, you need to set up a easy spreadsheet with the under statistics so you can with out trouble tune the transport of every of your purchaser's tasks.

•   Order variety

•   Client name or e mail

•   When your purchaser located the order

•   When you positioned the order on Fiverr

- Which freelancer you located the order with

- The timeline promised via the freelancer

- The timeline you promised the client

- Then upload two (2) timings inside the diverse begin and prevent date while you may test in with the freelancer and update your client in case you want to

- Where viable, moreover consist of on the same time as you will percent a number one view or minimum feasible product to your customer

6.2 Other guidelines that will help you control your orders

- Define a most kind of orders that you tackle

For a begin, only deal with maximum 2 or three responsibilities. Then as you end up more knowledgeable and cushty with the order manage, you may tackle greater.

- Always region the order on Fiverr within the equal day you got it from your client

Remember that your customer will rely your days from the time they location their order so do the entirety feasible to limit any lag between on the identical time as you get keep of the order and while you hire the freelancer. Another top notch concept is to deliver an acknowledgement e mail to the consumer notifying them that you have received the order and are running on turning in it by way of way of the specified lessen-off date.

Hello there, thanks for placing your order with _____ (employer call). Just preferred to verify that we've got received your order and function commenced going for walks on it. Please assume us to be finished through _____ (closing date). We will keep you updated on development and ship you regular updates but enjoy unfastened to also take a look at in with us and we may be satisfied to percentage with you a improvement update.

• Always upload 1 – 2 days to the real shipping timeline you supply your purchaser

Add a buffer of 1 – 2 days this allows you to ensure which you check the first-rate of the art work and can request a revision wherein the freelancer did no longer supply to the right degree of incredible earlier than you share with the client.

• Share any minimal possible concept along aspect your customer to limit amount of revisions

This is specifically right in case of layout paintings. For example, if you are making geared up a podcast cowl artwork, you might want to percent the difficult concept or cool animated film collectively at the side of your customer so you do now not spend the time doing the whole layout simplest for the patron to say they do no longer like how it appears. Remember in case you additionally percentage the idea with the customer, you co-private the venture as a result making the very last output lots extra amusing for the client.

Remember that you are handling multiple project and a couple of freelancers so ensure you do everything feasible to be organized and no longer lose track of any venture and its timelines

EFFECTIVE COMMUNICATION TIPS

Effective communique could make the difference amongst final and dropping a sale. In our revel in, we located that responding to patron enquiries indoors 1 – three hours lets in to electricity up your conversion fee significantly. Therefore, it is to your great hobby to make a communications plan that offers you this for you.

7.1 Communication pointers

- Take time to recognize your customer

Knowing and information your client's desires is important with a purpose to speak successfully with them. You do now not want to encounter as despite the fact that you are uncertain at the right ask out of your client.

For example, whilst you acquire an enquiry from a capability patron, rather than going earlier to prescribe a solution, begin through checking your statistics of the purchaser's hassle.

Hello _____ (client's name). Thank you for attaining out to us. I can be happy to help you.

If I understood your request successfully, you cited which you are searching out someone to do a smooth podcast cowl paintings layout that will help you collect your podcast proper proper right into a logo. If that's the case, then we may be satisfied to help you.

We offer a podcast cowl artwork format issuer...

• Use the proper conversation device

Using a ticketing device is better that using your simple email device due to the fact you can create one in every of a type agent names and create a reaction time desk that makes it appearance as notwithstanding the truth that you have were given were given a set of people sending via responses to clients on behalf of your commercial commercial enterprise employer. Longer time period, even as you hire a digital help to control the patron responses, you may additionally supply then a log in account to do this.

We choose to use Jira due to the reality it is free for up to three retailers. Meaning you may have 3 personas responding to your purchaser's emails in reality.

•   Track your communication and make certain you follow up with customers

Keep the conversation strains among you and your patron open and do now not look forward to your client to get lower back to you. A brief email reminder whilst you're looking forward to a response will assist you decorate your conversions. This is a few different gain of using a ticketing tool like Jira

With Jira, every time you ship an e-mail reaction to a patron, it adjustments the repute to "Waiting for Customer" permitting you to understand wherein you're anticipating responses and you could near tickets on the equal time as you're finished.

Remember no longer to be spammy. Keep your electronic mail reminders to maximum as quickly as a day, or wherein feasible even as quickly as each 3 days. This permits enough time on your patron to get back to you.

- Use easy language

Remember, now not all your clients apprehend the technical factors of the paintings. Therefore, as masses as feasible, use easy language.

- Use words like 'we' or 'us' to reveal togetherness

Using phrases like "we" or "us" shows the consumer that each of you're each within the identical institution.

- End each reaction with a query

Questions assist preserve the consumer engaged. So where feasible, quit every reaction with a question.

- Personalize each response

I can not stress the significance of personalizing each client reaction. This is the final way to expose that you apprehend your purchaser's desires and can offer them a customized answer.

- Create responses that you may without difficulty adapt and personalize

As a timesaver, put together a few responses to the regularly asked questions. These responses will allow you to shop time while responding to consumer enquiries. However, your canned responses want to depart room for personalisation so you can display the customer that you understand their goals.

POINT TO NOTE

Your customer might be evaluating a couple of groups and alternatives for them to get their artwork finished. Therefore, it's far important to reply:

- In a nicely timed way

- In a expert manner

- With as lots element as viable

- As sharply and immediately to the factor

7.2   How to speak with a difficult or sad client

You will come upon all sorts of clients, and it is inevitable that at some point, you will should deal with sad customers. Therefore, it's miles superb to put together yourself to realise the way to address them. Here are some tips that will help you address tough or sad customers.

• Listen attentively

Make wonderful you offer your client the possibility to air their worries and grievances. Start with a independent declaration like

"Please inform me why you're dissatisfied", or "Let's float over what happened." This subtly creates the road to your customer to understand that you are prepared and willing to pay attention.

Resist any temptation to treatment the client's hassle right away or to jump into stop. Make remarkable you in reality understand the purchaser's goals.

- Be empathic and express regret

Show the consumer which you understand why they're dissatisfied. "I sincerely apprehend why you feel this way", or "I completely apprehend the way you experience." Make terrific you make an apology for the problem as well.

"I am very sorry that we did now not get your art work completed on time, specifically on account that this is a part of the high-quality metrics we song in our industrial employer."

- Present a approach to them

Once you've got have been given allowed the patron to air their concerns and apologized for the hassle, that is your area to offer the consumer with a solution.

"I understand which you need the artwork thru the usage of the next day and we're walking past due in turning in. On my element, I will make certain we are do everything feasible to get this to you in the next 6 hours."

In case you aren't clean on the right option to offer the purchaser, you can provide them the power to resolve the scenario. Ask the consumer what ought to make them glad.

"If my proposed answer does now not provide you with the results you need, I would love to hear what is going to assist make this example better. If it's far in power then I gets it carried out, if now not, then we exercise some distinctive solution that works together."

- Act

Once you have were given agreed on an answer with the consumer, then make certain you put into effect it without delay. Explain to the customer the stairs that you could take to shut off the trouble.

After the state of affairs has been resolved, it is critical to conform with up with the patron and take a look at that they may be satisfied with the selection. Remember to express regret all all over again for the sooner trouble and provide them a discount on their subsequent purchase.

Use the remarks obtained from the patron to decorate your service transport. Find the inspiration of the trouble and ensure you restore it proper away. Use this to decorate your artwork practices and order control.

- Do you want to relook at your list of pre-acquainted freelancers?

- What processes do you want to relook to make sure this does not manifest over again?

TRACKING YOUR AGENCY'S PERFORMANCE

Tracking the general performance of your employer is critical to your fulfillment. By statistics your ordinary overall performance metrics, you can guard, optimize, and generate more leads on your commercial enterprise organization. This next economic disaster goes via the highlights of monitoring your drop servicing corporation's standard overall performance.

eight.1   Using Google Analytics to tune your internet website ordinary performance

Here are a few questions that you may have about your net internet site site visitors.

•   Track who is touring your website

•   How are they finding your net internet web page?

•   Which pages are they touchdown on as their first net web page?

•   How many pages do they go to in each session?

- How do they have interaction together with your content material cloth fabric?

- Are you principal them thru the income funnel?

- What pages have the very best conversion expenses?

You can use open supply structures like Google Analytics to song your performance.

This is eBook isn't centered at the technical elements. Therefore, we are able to not move into the facts of having your Google Analytics tracking set up. You can get masses of tutorials on-line that help you integrate the Google Analytics tracking together at the side of your WordPress or Shopify shop.

eight.2   Marketing spend standard overall performance

If you'll be producing leads the usage of the paid platform (which we simplest suggest as a secondary manner to generate leads), then you'll want to song your advertising and advertising spend. Some key metrics you may need to keep song of include your ad's click thru fee (CTR) and the flow returned on ad spend.

eight.2.1 Ad click on on-through-charge (CTR)

Your ad's click on thru price is a degree of how many clicks you get for the advert divided through manner of the overall quantity of impressions for the ad. Therefore, if your ad has 100 impressions and 3 people click on on it, your CTR is probably three%.

According to WordStream, the common CTR for Google Ads is 1.Nine% [6] at the same time as that of Facebook commercials is 1.6% [7].

The higher your click on through fee, the higher your advert's engagement. However, in case your ad's click on on through fee is manner decrease than the commonplace, this could mean you need to trade the advert itself as your ad's target market are not finding it to be applicable.

8.2.2 Conversion rate (CR)

Your conversion charge is the extensive sort of conversions or orders which you get divided via the complete amount of internet net page perspectives in your touchdown internet page. Assuming your net web page had one hundred perspectives and you acquire three profits; this would work out to a conversion price of 3%.

three% is the not unusual CR for online enterprise corporation company internet internet web sites [8]. If your conversion price is lower than three%, then this commonly suggests that there may be an problem along with your touchdown net web page. You should likely need to tweak your landing internet net web page the use of a number of the tips for an powerful touchdown net page that we furnished here in Chapter 4.2 - Tips for an effective touchdown web web page.

eight.2.Three Return on Ad Spend (ROAS)

Return on ad spend is the second one metric that we recommend you maintain a song on. Your ROAS is simply the gross revenue you get from your conversions divided via the usage of the value of your ad. For instance, if you purchased 10 clients who bought a bundle for $99 every, this may be a gross income of $990. If you spent $4 hundred to generate this sales, this shows your ROAS is 990 divided through the use of four hundred which equals to two.475.

In the only phrases, your ROAS shows how plenty you are making for each greenback you spend.

In this situation, you are making approximately $2.Five for every #1 you spend on marketing.

The average ROAS in keeping with a have a examine finished via Nielsen [9] is .Eight. Therefore, in case you are not generating $2.Eight for each $1 you spend on advertising and advertising and marketing, then you definitely definately actually want to relook at each your ad or your touchdown page.

TRACKING YOUR AGENCY'S FINANCIALS

Lack of proper financial document preserving is one of the top six (6) reasons why begin u.S.Fail. As a drop servicing industrial company corporation proprietor, if you are not on pinnacle of your enterprise company's financials, you're probable to fall into problems developing your corporation employer. Therefore, it's far important as a way to song your commercial enterprise agency's financials and on this phase, we display you a few pointers to ensure you're on top of your enterprise business enterprise's financials.

9.1   Tips to stay on path of your employer's financials

•   Ensure you document your income and fees on each order

It is important that you tune your profits and fees. This lets in you recognize whether or not or not or no longer each undertaking is worthwhile or not. Have a clean excel sheet that tracks the under:

• Gross Income (the quantity your consumer paid)

• Net profits (after fee processing prices charged with the aid of PayPal, Stripe, or Shopify)

• Project associated fees

o How an lousy lot you paid the freelancer?

o Any financial institution prices for sending rate to the freelancer

• Marketing prices - how a bargain you spent for your advertisements bypass all systems.

Better to tune those on a weekly or monthly basis and cut up up the value for the duration of the entire orders you obtained.

Alternatively, you could set up your Facebook Pixel or Google Analytics E-Commerce Tracking to get your charge in step with purchase and use this because the determine to your cost consistent with conversion.

• Keep reviewing your charges (mainly marketing expenses)

Keep tracking your prices and tweaking as great as possible to get them to be decrease. The lower your price in keeping with buy, the higher your profitability.

- Stay on top of your business company seasonality

Remember that there can be some shape of seasonality in your profits. For example, within the direction of the vacations, you'll have just a few clients ordering your services. Therefore, exceptional to devise around this and probably offer some reductions after the holidays to get your commercial agency decrease back to boom.

- Keep song of any loans you have got were given were given

Make satisfactory you keep accurate facts of every what you owe and what others owe you. Make certain you keep up together with your bills on those and that you issue them in as you are making your payouts.

- Keep a separate account on your commercial employer

Mixing your commercial enterprise income and your non-public earnings is a recipe for disaster. It is crucial to keep your industrial agency earnings separate because it will assist you song your industrial employer charges one after the other and will also assist you land this subsequent tip.

- Make superb you pay your self first

Since you are the precept employee for the company, make sure you region apart cash to pay your self. Start with a sincere price, as an example taking 10% of the internet earnings of your organization. Then go away the ninety% for growing your industrial company. Then slowly, you could boom this determine to 30% or perhaps 50% of the internet profits.

As your drop servicing business agency grows, set your self a revenue and draw out this quantity monthly regardless of how a whole lot your profits is. This hassle will assist you make bigger your commercial business enterprise extra sustainably.

Then each quarter, you could pay your self an advantage of as lots as 30% of the business corporation' income.

The remaining 70% will assist pay your earnings and that of various employees like your virtual assistants even when your commercial organization is in off-season.

LIVING THE LIFE OF A SUCCESSFUL BUSINESS OWNER

10.1   Tips to live the life of a a achievement enterprise company proprietor

• Create a domestic place of business

Identify a vicinity that is free from clutter and distraction and wherein you may be most green.

• Create a work time table and outline your working hours

Create a plan for 1 – 2 hours in that you do your advertising and advertising and advertising sports (e.G. Responding to questions on Quora or Reddit), take a look at in with freelancers at the improvement of your orders, check the overall basic performance of your advertising and marketing campaigns and tweak wherein important.

• Make nice you leave sufficient time for retaining song of your debts and taxes

As indicated in Chapter 9.1 - Tips to live heading inside the right path of your commercial organisation organization's financials, it's miles important to maintain song of your business enterprise financials. So, in your time table, leave sufficient time to tune your commercial enterprise earnings and prices, make all vital bills on behalf of your organisation, and live on route of your taxes. If you're hiring someone to do that for you, use this time to check on what they're doing for you.

• Document what works

Make sure you report which of the tweaks that you implement facilitates to generate lower price consistent with buy, higher click on via fees, or better conversion charges on your touchdown pages. This makes positive you could outcomes replicate in case you want to sell greater offerings.

Chapter 9: How To Find Clients For

Your Business

Now that you have your shop up and walking, you'll want some customers that will help you pay the bills. You can land clients thru relying on unfastened or paid leads. Free leads aren't constantly unfastened, it genuinely means that you are shopping for the ones leads collectively together along with your time, in preference in your cash.

In this next phase, we talk in detail the way to land free and paid leads using actionable examples in case you need to expand your drop servicing business enterprise.

5.1   Free leads

Free leads are essentially leads which you pay for the use of your difficult work. What this indicates is that thru supporting the customers find out you and using website online visitors on your net web site, they likely become your clients. In this section, we speak the manner to generate loose leads.

Paying for leads must be your 2nd preference if you need to increase your organisation sustainably. This is due to the truth for every free lead you generate, you spend nothing in advertising charges because of this turning in a better income for your business business business enterprise in contrast to paid leads in which you want to invest inside the industrial and therefore making your margins thinner.

Many companies give up on unfastened leads because the ones take time to construct. Remember, that is the most sustainable way to broaden your business employer.

If you draw close getting unfastened leads, you will be capable of be greater a success in your corporation long term.

It is like planting a fruit tree. It can also take an prolonged while for the seedling to grow, but, at the same time as it does achieve adulthood, you may harvest for lots, a few years.

five.1.1   Generate free leads the usage of your weblog

It isn't any mystery that starting your private weblog enables you show off your expertise and to installation yourself as an expert on your vicinity of hobby. Whenever you positioned up on your blog, you furthermore may also make your self greater credible for your functionality customers thinking about that they could take a look at content material cloth which you have posted on the best trouble they are managing and the answer you offer. The notable element is that your weblog posts do no longer always want to be very lengthy.

In blogging, the counseled manner is to prioritize amount over duration. Prioritize generating greater short articles over writing few portions of content material material which might be prolonged and unique. Here are 3 expert hints to get your blog to generate leads in your industrial organisation.

1. Do your studies – ensure you do key-phrase studies using on-line key-word equipment together with Answer The Public (answerthepublic.Com), and Google Keyword Planner. This will help you recognize which key phrases to goal your posts on and to prioritize your content material material.

2. Provide particular rate. Do no longer motive to duplicate and paste content material that is available on special net web sites. What particular content material are you able to offer? Think approximately giving use times in which your clients have used your offerings to treatment their issues. You also can speak the not unusual problems that clients face and the way you could help them clear up those troubles.

three. The final tip is to prevent your weblog located up with a name-to-motion. Since the blog post is your marketing and advertising and marketing tool, ensure to characteristic your name-to-movement (CTA) on the end. This will make the positioned up actionable. Try different call-to-moves from asking customers to move away a commentary within the occasion that they have got a completely unique project they'll be dealing with, or an real call-to-movement that leads them to purchase your provider.

5.1.2 Generating unfastened leads on social media

By posting to your social media pages, you are also installing your self as an expert inside the location of interest. You can grow your network via manner of posting applicable content material fabric cloth as a way to have interaction your functionality patron. Here, I should endorse using the rule of four to at least one. This approach that post four (4) quantities of useful content material material material for each one (1) piece of advertising cloth.

Therefore, whilst making your content material plan, ensure you have were given a lineup of beneficial articles and specific content material in advance than you insert your marketing and advertising fabric.

Facebook is frequently the exquisite platform for changing leads for B2B groups. Followed by way of way of LinkedIn and Instagram. Therefore, prioritize these 3 (three) social networks to your social media plan to make certain that you can successfully intention the proper purpose market.

Simple sports activities encompass:

1. Optimizing your social media profiles — make sure you've got were given your

emblems uploaded, your description installation, and speak to facts.

2. Create your name-to-motion – remember your social media net web page is likewise an effective touchdown internet page. Therefore, make sure you have got your name-to-motion installation effectively.

3. Make your content material attractive – supply people a purpose to percent and engage together along side your content material. You can also want to provide time-constrained reductions or coupons or invite capability customers to join your e mail ebook or webinars.

Consider furthermore tourist posting. Can you write an editorial for a few other weblog in exchange for the opposite blogger writing a piece of writing in your weblog?

5.1.Three Generating free leads using influencers

Influencer advertising is a tactic that will help you broaden your following and consequently help you show off your offerings to the right purpose marketplace. In this example, we aren't speaking about paying influencers to percent your content cloth. No, we're talking approximately using influencer content to broaden your network.

1. Reshare influencer content material fabric cloth to your network as concept-control portions.

2. Some influencers can be inclined to offer a shout out to their fanatics in trade for a discount to your employer.

three. Mention influencer content material to your internet web site content material material. However, be careful now not to generate horrible PR to your business business enterprise via making it appear as despite the fact that your organization and the influencer are in a partnership.

When the use of influencers, it's far excellent to discover micro-influencers in vicinity of macro-influencers. Micro-influencer refers to influencers which have amongst 1,000 to one hundred,000 fanatics. Because in their decrease following, micro-influencers force higher engagement and they will pressure greater conversions for you.

five.1.Four Generating unfastened leads by using using manner of bloodless emailing

If you belief e mail marketing is vain, you couldn't be extra incorrect. Email stays one of the super strategies to generate unfastened leads. There is even a time period, "the paintings of cold emailing" this is used to reveal the high-quality way to generate leads using electronic mail. Basically, it all comes proper all the way down to being easy, at once to the issue, and personalizing every e-mail which you draft.

To generate leads using bloodless emails you have to hold in thoughts finding the proper leads to email. You can do this both through having an pick-in shape on your internet site or reaching out to capacity clients and sending them emails.

Using the instance of selling podcast cowl art, you will do a are searching for for for your desired are attempting to find engine, as an instance, for podcasts in Boston, you then definately honestly ought to electronic mail the podcast proprietors via using their touch bureaucracy, or as an opportunity attaining out to them via their social media pages. Make first-rate to apply the direct messaging characteristic on social media in place of posting public feedback on their posts. This is due to the reality you need to reach out to them right now for this reason searching greater expert, in desire to searching determined through posting a public commentary.